中学英語で読んでみる

イラスト
英英
英単語

ジャパンタイムズ出版 英語出版編集部 &
ロゴポート 編

JN112610

the japan times 出版

はじめに

　皆さんは、英英辞典を使ったことがありますか？　「学校の先生に勧められたけど、ハードルが高くて手が出せていない」、「引いてはみたけれど、意味がわからないのでやめた」…という人もいるかもしれませんね。

　英語を引くとすぐに日本語の訳が出てくる英和辞典と違い、知らない単語を英英辞典で調べると、説明の英文にも知らない単語が出てきて、今度はその単語を引き…という無限ループにはまってしまう恐れがあります。ですから英英辞典は、「まずは自分の知っている単語から調べてみる」のがポイントです。

　例えばelephantという単語。動物の「ゾウ」であることは皆さんもご存じでしょう。そう、「大きくて、鼻が長くて、牙のはえているあの動物」です。英語では、An elephant is a very large animal with a long, flexible nose and two long tusks.（ゾウは、長くてしなやかな鼻と2本の長い牙を持つ、とても大きな動物です）のように説明することができます。これならflexible（よく曲がる、しなやかな）やtusk（牙）という単語を知らなくても、皆さんのゾウについて持っている知識やイメージから、説明文の意味を推測することができますね。逆に、flexibleやtuskという単語をリアルにイメージしながら覚えることもできるというわけです。

本書『中学英語で読んでみる イラスト英英英単語』では、elephant（ゾウ）や giraffe（キリン）などの動物のほか、sea（海）、hand（手）、table（テーブル）、spoon（スプーン）、hotel（ホテル）、sandwich（サンドイッチ）といった、主に中学卒業レベルの身近な250ほどの単語を場面別に取り上げ、かわいらしいイラストとともに英語の説明をつけました。ときどき知らない単語が出てくるかもしれませんが、心配はご無用です！英語の説明のすぐ下に訳もつけたので、安心して読み進めてください。

　この本を読んで、「英語を英語で理解するのって面白いな」と思っていただけたら幸いです。そして、「もっと英語を英語で理解してみたい！」と思ったら、本書の姉妹編である『英英英単語』シリーズ、そして英英辞典ものぞいてみてください。きっとあなたの英語学習の強い味方になってくれるはずです。

編者

目次

本書の構成と使い方

本書は、英語を英語のまま理解できるようになりたい、これから英英辞典を使ってみたいと考えている方のための単語集です。私たちになじみのある244語を14の場面に分けてご紹介しています。

1 場面イラスト

その場面に登場するすべての見出し語が描かれたイラストです。
どんな単語が登場するか、イラストと一緒に見ておきましょう。

2 見出し語

アメリカつづりを採用しています。イギリスつづりが異なる場合は注記に挙げています。

3 発音記号

アメリカ発音を採用しています。

4 見出し語のイラスト

見出し語を描いたイラストです。

5 訳語

見出し語の品詞と訳語です。

6 英語の語義説明

見出し語の語義を英語で説明しています。説明中の見出し語は太字になっています。

7 語義説明の訳

英語の語義説明の訳です。

8 注記

見出し語の複数形・類義語・関連語、見出し語が動詞の場合はその活用など、さまざまな補足情報を掲載しています。

9 音声のトラック番号

音声には見出し語と英語の語義説明が収録されています。音声は付属CDで再生できるほか、アプリまたはPCでダウンロードして聞くこともできます。ご利用方法は010ページをご覧ください。

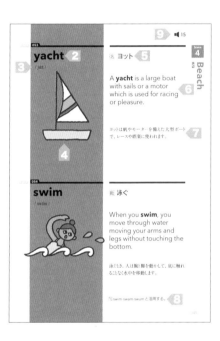

053
yacht
/ jɑt /

名 ヨット

Scene **4** Beach 砂浜

A **yacht** is a large boat with sails or a motor which is used for racing or pleasure.

ヨットは帆やモーターを備えた大型ボートで、レースや娯楽に使われます。

054
swim
/ swɪm /

動 泳ぐ

When you **swim**, you move through water moving your arms and legs without touching the bottom.

泳ぐとき、人は腕と脚を動かして、底に触れることなく水中を移動します。

注 swim-swam-swum と活用する。

本書で使われている記号

〈 〉…他動詞の目的語を表します。

（ ）…訳語の補足説明です。

名 …名詞

動 …動詞

巻末ボキャブラリーチェック

巻末に、確認のための問題を用意しています。ヒントを参考に、語義説明が表す英単語のつづりを完成させましょう。わからない場合は元のページに戻って確認しましょう。

英語の語義説明を読むヒント

英語の語義説明を読むときに知っておくと便利なポイントをいくつかご紹介します。

1 「〜を持った」「〜のついた」を表すwith

前置詞のwithは「〜と一緒に」という意味で覚えていることが多いですが、英英辞典では「〜を持った」「〜のついた」という意味でよく使われます。

例 A giraffe is a very tall animal **with** a very long neck and legs.

> キリンは、とても長い首と脚を持つ、非常に背の高い動物です。

2 関係代名詞のwhich

関係代名詞のwhichも多用されます。(whichの代わりにthatを使う辞書もありますが、直前に前置詞がつく場合はthatは使えません。)

例 An airplane is a vehicle **which** flies through the air.

> 飛行機は、空を飛ぶ乗り物です。

The Earth is the planet **on which** we live.

> 地球は、私たちが住む惑星です。

3 「人一般」を表すyou

英英辞典ではよく「人一般」を表すのにyouという語が使われます。この本でもこの用法のyouを使っています。(このyouは「あなた」という意味ではありません。)

またsomeoneなどの不定代名詞の代用としてthey(their、themも含む)を使う場合もあります。

例 When **you** pay an amount of money to someone, **you** give it to **them** for something **you** buy from **them**.

> 誰かにある額のお金を支払うとき、人はその人から買うものの代金として、その人にその金額を渡します。

知っておきたい！本書の100%活用術

本書を使った学習法をいくつかご紹介します。

1　イラストを見ながら、見出し語と語義説明を読んでみましょう

本書で取り上げた見出し語は、ほとんど皆さんの知っているものばかり。まずはイラストを見ながら英語の語義説明を読んでみましょう。理解できない部分がある場合は、下の訳を参考にしてください。

2　英語らしい表現に注目しましょう

語義説明を読むときは、英語らしい表現に着目しましょう。例えば、arm（腕）という単語は、タコの「足」を表したり、いすやソファーの「ひじかけ」の意味でも使われます。また、常に複数形で使う単語や、可算名詞と不可算名詞を意識しながら読むと、英語的な感覚をつかむのに役立ちます。

3　音声を利用しましょう

前述の学習法に音声も加えましょう。語義説明を見ながら音声を聞き、自分でも発音してみるとより身につきます。

4　巻末ボキャブラリーチェックを繰り返し解きましょう

正解できるようになるまで、巻末ボキャブラリーチェックを繰り返し解きましょう。語義説明を何度も読むことは、言い換え（パラフレージング）力の強化につながります。

音声のご利用案内

本書の音声は、付属CDで再生できるほか、スマートフォン（アプリ）やパソコンを通じてMP3形式でダウンロードし、ご利用いただくことができます。

 ## スマートフォン

1. ジャパンタイムズ出版の音声アプリ「OTO Navi」をインストール

2. 「OTO Navi」で本書を検索

3. 「OTO Navi」で音声をダウンロードし、再生
   ※3秒早送り・早戻し、繰り返し再生などの便利機能つき。学習にお役立てください。

 ## パソコン

1. ブラウザからジャパンタイムズ出版のサイト「BOOK CLUB」にアクセス
   https://bookclub.japantimes.co.jp/book/b583273.html

2. 「ダウンロード」ボタンをクリック

3. 音声をダウンロードし、iTunesなどに取り込んで再生
   ※音声は zipファイルを展開（解凍）してご利用ください。

Scene

1

Savanna / Desert

サバンナ／砂漠

zebra

elephant

grass

watch

leopard

giraffe

lion

ostrich

□□□ **001**

elephant

/ éləfənt /

名 ゾウ

An **elephant** is a very large animal with a long, flexible nose and two long tusks. Elephants live in Africa and Asia.

ゾウは、長くてしなやかな鼻と2本の長い牙を持つ、とても大きな動物です。ゾウはアフリカとアジアに住んでいます。

✐「ゾウの鼻」はtrunkと言う。tusk（牙）を作る物質がivory（象牙）。flexibleは「よく曲がる、しなやかな」という意味。

□□□ **002**

zebra

/ zíːbrə /

名 シマウマ

A **zebra** is an African animal which looks like a horse. Zebras have black and white stripes all over their bodies.

シマウマはアフリカの動物で、ウマのように見えます。シマウマは体全体に黒と白のしま模様があります。

✐複数形はzebrasあるいはzebra。

□□ **003**

lion

/ láɪən /

名 ライオン

A **lion** is a strong animal which looks like a large cat with golden brown fur. Lions live mainly in Africa.

ライオンは、きつね色の毛皮を持つ、大きな猫のように見える強い動物です。ライオンは主にアフリカに住んでいます。

💡「メスのライオン」は lioness、「子ライオン」は lion cub と言う。

□□ **004**

leopard

/ lépərd /

名 ヒョウ

A **leopard** is a large golden brown cat with black spots. Leopards live in southern Asia and Africa.

ヒョウは、黒い斑点のある大きなきつね色の猫です。ヒョウは南アジアとアフリカに住んでいます。

□□□ **005**

giraffe

/ ʤəræf /

名 **キリン**

A **giraffe** is a very tall animal with a very long neck and legs. Giraffes live in Africa and eat leaves and buds on trees.

キリンは、とても長い首と脚を持つ、非常に背の高い動物です。キリンはアフリカに住んでいて、木の葉や芽を食べます。

✐複数形はgiraffesあるいはgiraffe。budは「芽」という意味。

□□□ **006**

ostrich

/ ɑ́:strɪʧ /

名 **ダチョウ**

An **ostrich** is a very large African bird with a long neck and legs. Ostriches run very fast but cannot fly.

ダチョウは、長い首と脚を持つとても大きなアフリカの鳥です。ダチョウはとても速く走りますが、飛ぶことはできません。

---

007 □□

grass
/ grǽs /

名 草

Grass is a plant with thin green leaves. Grass covers the ground in fields and is often eaten by animals.

草は、薄くて緑色の葉を持つ植物です。草は野原の地面を覆い、しばしば動物の食料になります。

---

008 □□

watch
/ wάːtʃ /

動 ～を見る、観察する

When you **watch** someone or something, you look at them, usually for a period of time, paying attention to what is happening.

人やものを観察するとき、人はふつうしばらくの間、起こっていることに注意を払いながら、それらを見ます。

📝pay attention to は「～に注意する」という意味。

□□□ **009**

camel

/ kǽml /

名 ラクダ

A **camel** is a large animal with a long neck and one or two large lumps on its back. Camels carry people and goods in the desert.

ラクダは、首が長く背中に1つまたは2つの大きなこぶのある大きな動物です。ラクダは砂漠で人やものを運びます。

✐lumpは「こぶ」という意味。特にラクダなどの動物の背の「こぶ」はhumpと言う。

□□□ **010**

cactus

/ kǽktəs /

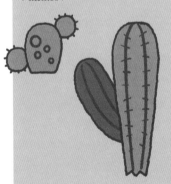

名 サボテン

A **cactus** is a plant which grows in the desert. Cacti have a lot of sharp points instead of leaves.

サボテンは、砂漠で育つ植物です。サボテンには葉の代わりに多くの鋭いとげがあります。

✐複数形はcacti / kǽktaɪ / あるいはcactuses。

□□ **011**

oasis

/ ouéisis /

名 オアシス

An **oasis** is a small area in the desert where there is water and plants can grow.

オアシスは、水があって植物が育つことのできる、砂漠の小さな場所です。

複数形は oases / ouéisiːz /。

□□ **012**

sand

/ sǽnd /

名 砂

Sand is very small, loose pieces of rock. Sand is found on beaches, in deserts, etc.

砂は、とても小さくサラサラした岩の断片です。砂は浜辺や砂漠などに見られます。

□□□ 013

sky

/ skáɪ /

名 空

The sky is the space over the Earth where you can see the sun, the moon, stars, and clouds.

空は、太陽、月、星、雲が見える地球の上方の空間です。

□□□ 014

ride

/ ráɪd /

動 ～に乗る

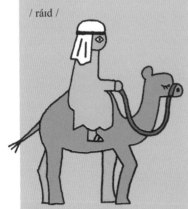

When you **ride** an animal, you sit on it and control its movements as it moves.

人が動物に乗るとき、人はそれに座り、それが移動するのに合わせて動きをコントロールします。

✐ ride-rode-ridden と活用する。

Scene

2

Jungle
ジャングル

fly

banana

monkey

parrot

snake

gorilla

□□□ **015**

gorilla

/ gərílə /

名 ゴリラ

A **gorilla** is a very strong animal like a large monkey. Gorillas live in African forests.

ゴリラは、大きなサルのような、とても強い動物です。ゴリラはアフリカの森に住んでいます。

🖉 gorilla や chimpanzee（チンパンジー）などの「類人猿」を ape と言う。

□□□ **016**

monkey

/ mʌ́ŋki /

名 サル

A **monkey** is an animal which is like a person in shape. Monkeys have long tails and climb trees.

サルは、人のような姿をした動物です。サルには長いしっぽがあり、木に登ります。

🖉 monkey と ape は学術上区別される。

017

sloth

/ slɔ́:θ /

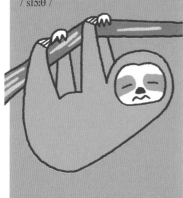

名 ナマケモノ

A **sloth** is an animal which lives in trees and moves very slowly. Sloths live in the tropical rainforests.

ナマケモノは木の上に住んでいて、とても ゆっくりと動く動物です。ナマケモノは熱帯 雨林に住んでいます。

018

snake

/ snéik /

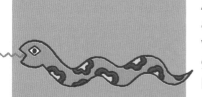

名 ヘビ

A **snake** is a long, thin animal with no legs which slides along the ground. Some snakes are poisonous.

ヘビは脚のない細長い動物で、地面を はって進みます。ヘビの中には毒を持つも のもいます。

📝 poisonousは「毒(poison)のある」という 意味。

□□□ **019**

frog

/ frɑ́:g /

名 **カエル**

A **frog** is a small animal which lives both in water and on land. Frogs have long back legs for jumping.

カエルは、水中と陸上の両方に住む小動物です。カエルには跳ねるための長い後ろ脚があります。

□□□ **020**

parrot

/ pǽrət /

名 **オウム**

A **parrot** is a tropical bird with a curved beak and brightly-colored feathers. Some parrots can be taught to copy human speech.

オウムは、曲がったくちばしと鮮やかな色の羽を持つ熱帯の鳥です。オウムの中には、人の言葉をまねるよう教えることができるものもいます。

✐beakは「くちばし」という意味。

021

trunk

/ tríŋk /

名 幹

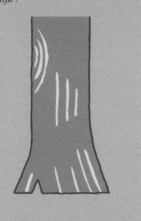

The **trunk** of a tree is the thick main stem from which the branches grow.

木の幹は太い主要な茎で、そこから枝が生えます。

📖「ゾウの鼻」と同じ語。stem については p. 126 参照。

022

branch

/ bréntʃ /

名 枝

The **branches** of a tree are parts which grow out from the trunk and have leaves, flowers, fruit, or smaller branches growing on them.

木の枝は幹から伸びる部分で、そこからは葉や花、実、小さな枝が生えます。

□□□ **023**

vine

/ váɪn /

名 つる、つる草

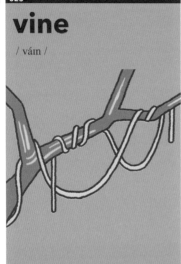

A **vine** is a plant which has very long stems. Vines grow up and around something, such as a tree.

つるは、とても長い茎を持つ植物です。つるは木のようなものに巻きついて伸びていきます。

□□□ **024**

crocodile

/ krάːkədὰɪl /

名 ワニ

A **crocodile** is a large animal which has a long body, thick skin, and a long mouth with sharp teeth. Crocodiles live in rivers or lakes in warm climates.

ワニは、長い体、厚い皮、鋭い歯のある長い口を持つ大きな動物です。ワニは温暖な気候の土地の川や湖に住んでいます。

□□ **025**

river

/ rívər /

名 川

A **river** is a large natural flow of water. Rivers cross an area of land toward a lake, ocean, etc.

川は、大きな自然の水の流れです。川は湖や海などの方へと大地を横切っていきます。

□□ **026**

banana

/ bənǽnə /

名 バナナ

A **banana** is a long curved tropical fruit with a thick peel which is yellow when it is ripe.

バナナは長く曲がった熱帯の果物で、厚い皮は熟すと黄色になります。

✐peelは「(果物などの)皮」、ripeは「熟した」という意味。

□□□ **027**

hang

/ hǽŋ /

動 ぶら下がる

When something **hangs** in a high place, it is attached there so that it does not touch the ground.

ものが高いところにぶら下がっているとき、それは地面に触れないように、その場所にくっついています。

 hang-hung-hungと活用する。

□□□ **028**

fly

/ flάɪ /

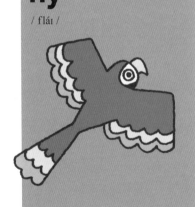

動 飛ぶ

When something such as a bird or insect **flies**, it moves through the air using wings.

鳥や昆虫などが飛ぶとき、それは羽を使って空中を移動します。

✐ fly-flew-flownと活用する。

Scene

3

Countryside / Farm

田舎／農場

paint

field

milk

mole

egg

mouse

☐☐☐ **029**

horse

/ hɔ́:rs /

名 ウマ

A **horse** is a large animal with long legs and hooves. Horses are used for riding and for carrying or pulling heavy things.

ウマは、長い脚とひづめのある大きな動物です。ウマは乗ったり、重いものを運んだり引っ張ったりするのに使われます。

🖉 hoof（複数形は hooves）は「ひづめ」という意味。ウマやライオンの「たてがみ」は mane と言う。

☐☐☐ **030**

cow

/ káʊ /

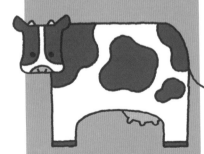

名 メウシ

A **cow** is a large female animal which is kept on farms for its milk or meat.

メウシは、牛乳や肉のために農場で飼育される大きなメスの動物です。

🖉「オウシ」は bull、「子ウシ」は calf、「牛肉」は beef と言う。

□□ **031**

sheep

/ ʃíːp /

名 ヒツジ

A **sheep** is an animal with long, curly hair. Sheep are raised on farms for their wool or meat.

ヒツジは、長い巻き毛のある動物です。ヒツジは羊毛や肉のために農場で飼育されます。

✐複数形もsheep。「子ヒツジ」はlambと言う。

□□ **032**

pig

/ píg /

名 ブタ

A **pig** is a fat animal with a wide, flat nose and a short, curly tail. Pigs are raised on farms for their meat.

ブタは、広くて平らな鼻と短く巻いたしっぽのある太った動物です。ブタは肉のために農場で飼育されます。

✐「豚肉」はporkと言う。

□□□ **033**

chicken

/ tʃíkɪn /

图 ニワトリ

A **chicken** is a bird which is raised on farms for its eggs or meat.

ニワトリは、卵や肉のために農場で飼育される鳥です。

✐「鶏肉」もchickenと言うが、その場合は不可算名詞。

□□□ **034**

duck

/ dʌ́k /

图 アヒル

A **duck** is a common bird which lives on or near water. Ducks have webbed feet for swimming and a flat beak.

アヒルは、水上または水辺に住む日常的な鳥です。アヒルには泳ぐための水かきのある足と、平らなくちばしがあります。

✐webbedは「(足に)水かきがある」という意味。

□□ 035

milk

/ mílk /

图 ミルク、乳

Milk is the white liquid which comes from female animals, such as cows. It is used as a drink or in cooking.

ミルクは、メウシなどのメスの動物から得られる白い液体です。飲み物として、あるいは料理に使われます。

□□ 036

egg

/ ég /

图 卵

An **egg** is a hard-shelled oval thing from which a young bird is born. Eggs are also eaten as food.

卵は硬い殻を持つ楕円形のもので、そこからひなが生まれます。また卵は食べ物として食べられます。

📎 ovalは「楕円形の、卵形の」という意味。

□□□ **037**

mole

/ móʊl /

名 モグラ

A **mole** is a small animal with dark gray fur. Moles are almost blind and dig tunnels under the ground to live in.

モグラは、濃い灰色の毛皮を持つ小動物です。モグラはほとんど目が見えず、地下にトンネルを掘ってそこに住んでいます。

□□□ **038**

mouse

/ máʊs /

名 ネズミ

A **mouse** is a small animal with a pointed nose and a long, thin tail. Mice live in houses or fields.

ネズミは、とがった鼻と細長いしっぽを持つ小動物です。ネズミは人家や畑に住んでいます。

複数形は mice / máɪs /。

field

/ fíːld /

名 畑

A **field** is an area of open land without trees or buildings. Fields are often used to grow crops or keep animals.

畑は、木や建物のない開けた土地の区域です。多くの場合、作物を育てたり動物を飼ったりするのに使われます。

✐ ここでのopenは「広々とした、開けた」という意味。

pond

/ páːnd /

名 池

A **pond** is an area of still, fresh water which is smaller than a lake. Ponds can be either natural or artificial.

池は、湖よりも小さく、流れていない淡水の区域です。自然のものも人工のものもあります。

✐ stillは「動かない、流れていない」という意味。

□□□ **041**

fence

/ féns /

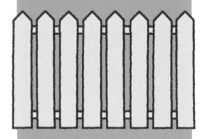

名 柵

A **fence** is a structure made of wood or metal supported by posts. Fences separate two areas of land.

柵は、支柱で支えられた木製あるいは金属製の構造物です。柵は2つの区域の土地を隔てます。

□□□ **042**

paint

/ péint /

動 〜を塗る

When you **paint** a wall or an object, you put paint on it to change its color.

壁やものを塗るとき、人はその上に塗料を塗って色を変えます。

✐ 「塗料、ペンキ」という名詞の意味もある。

Scene

4

Beach

浜辺

sea

/ síː /

名 海

The sea is the salt water which covers much of the Earth's surface.

海は、地球の表面の多くの部分を覆う塩水です。

🖉 ocean とも言う。

wave

/ wéɪv /

名 波

A **wave** is a line of raised water which moves across the surface of the sea.

波は、海面を横切って移動する隆起した水の線です。

045

island

/ áɪlənd /

名 **島**

An **island** is a piece of land which is completely surrounded by water.

島は、完全に水に囲まれた陸地です。

046

airplane

/ éərplèɪn /

名 **飛行機**

An **airplane** is a vehicle which flies through the air. Airplanes have wings and one or more engines.

飛行機は、空を飛ぶ乗り物です。翼と1つまたは複数のエンジンがあります。

単にplaneとも言う。vehicleは「乗り物、車両」という意味。

□□□ **047**

cloud

/ kláʊd /

名 雲

A **cloud** is a gray or white mass which floats in the sky. Clouds are made of very small drops of water.

雲は、空に浮かぶ灰色または白色のかたまりです。雲はとても小さな水滴でできています。

□□□ **048**

octopus

/ á:ktəpəs /

名 タコ

An **octopus** is a sea animal which has a soft round body and eight long arms. Octopuses are used for food.

タコは、柔らかくて丸い体と8本の長い腕を持つ海の動物です。タコは食用にされます。

📝 複数形は octopuses あるいは octopi / á:ktəpàɪ /。タコの「足」は英語では arm と言う。

049

crab
/ krǽb /

名 カニ

A **crab** is a sea animal which has a hard shell, eight legs, and two large claws. Crabs usually walk sideways on land.

カニは、硬い殻と8本の脚と2つの大きなはさみを持つ海の動物です。カニはふつう、陸では横向きに歩きます。

✓ claw は「(エビ・カニの)はさみ、(動物や鳥の)かぎ爪」という意味。

050

turtle
/ tə́ːrtl /

名 カメ

A **turtle** is an animal which has a hard shell covering its soft body and mainly lives in water.

カメは、柔らかい体を覆う硬い殻を持ち、主に水中に住む動物です。

✓「ウミガメ」は sea turtle、「リクガメ」は tortoise と言う。

□□□ **051**

clam
/ klǽm /

图 **二枚貝**

A **clam** is an animal with a soft body and a shell made of two parts which open and close. Clams live underwater and can be eaten.

二枚貝は、柔らかい体と開閉する2つの部分からなる殻を持つ動物です。二枚貝は水中に住んでいて、食べられます。

✐ ハマグリ・アサリなどを指す。

□□□ **052**

dolphin
/ dá:lfin /

图 **イルカ**

A **dolphin** is a very intelligent sea animal. Dolphins look like large fish but they breathe air. Dolphins are often friendly toward humans.

イルカは、とても知能の高い海の動物です。イルカは大きな魚のように見えますが、肺呼吸します。イルカは人間に対してしばしば友好的です。

□□ 053

yacht

/ jáːt /

名 ヨット

A **yacht** is a large boat with sails or a motor which is used for racing or pleasure.

ヨットは帆やモーターを備えた大型ボートで、レースや娯楽に使われます。

1□ 054

swim

/ swím /

動 泳ぐ

When you **swim**, you move through water moving your arms and legs without touching the bottom.

泳ぐとき、人は腕と脚を動かして、底に触れることなく水中を移動します。

swim-swam-swum と活用する。

□□□ **055**

fish

/ fiʃ /

動 釣りをする

When you **fish**, you try to catch fish with a fishing rod, nets, etc., either for food or as recreation.

釣りをするとき、人は釣り竿や網などで、食用にあるいは娯楽として魚を捕まえようとします。

□□□ **056**

surf

/ sɔ́ːrf /

動 サーフィンをする

When you **surf**, you ride on waves in the ocean on a surfboard.

サーフィンをするとき、人はサーフボードで海の波に乗ります。

Scene

5

Camping

キャンプ

lake

boat

backpack

rabbit

bike

□□□ 057

mountain

/ máʊntn /

名 山

A **mountain** is a very high hill, often with rocks near the top and steep sides.

山とはとても高い丘で、しばしば頂上付近に岩があり、険しい斜面を持っています。

□□□ 058

tent

/ tént /

名 テント

A **tent** is a portable shelter made of canvas, nylon, etc. which is supported by poles and ropes. Tents are often used for camping.

テントはキャンバス地やナイロンなどで作られた携帯用のシェルターで、支柱とロープで支えられます。テントはよくキャンプで使います。

17

□□ 059

fire

/ fáɪər /

名 火

Fire is the flames, heat, and light produced by burning.

火は、燃焼によって生じる炎、熱、および光です。

□□ 060

chat

/ tʃǽt /

動 おしゃべりをする

When people **chat**, they talk to each other in an informal and friendly way.

人々がおしゃべりするとき、彼らは形式ばらず、気さくに話し合います。

□□□ **061**

lake

/ léɪk /

名 湖

A **lake** is a large area of water which is surrounded by land.

湖は、陸に囲まれた広い水域です。

□□□ **062**

boat

/ bóʊt /

名 ボート

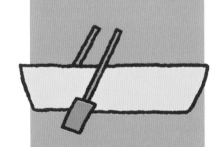

A **boat** is a small vehicle for traveling on water. Boats are usually smaller than ships and are moved by sails, oars, or motors.

ボートは、水上を移動するための小さな乗り物です。ボートはふつう船よりも小さく、帆、オール、またはモーターで動きます。

18

063

rabbit

/ rǽbət /

名 ウサギ

A **rabbit** is a small animal with long ears. Rabbits have long back legs for running and jumping. They live in holes under the ground.

ウサギは、耳の長い小動物です。ウサギは走ったり跳ねたりするための長い後ろ脚を持っています。地下の穴に住んでいます。

064

owl

/ áʊl /

名 フクロウ

An **owl** is a bird which has large round eyes, a sharp beak, and strong, sharp claws. Owls usually hunt small animals at night.

フクロウは、大きな丸い目、鋭いくちばし、そして強くて鋭いかぎ爪を持つ鳥です。フクロウはふつう夜に小動物を狩ります。

□□□ 065

spider

/ spáɪdər /

名 クモ

A **spider** is a small animal with eight legs. Spiders create webs to catch insects for food.

クモは、8本の脚を持つ小動物です。クモはえさにする昆虫を捕まえるために巣を作ります。

□□□ 066

chair

/ tʃéər /

名 いす

A **chair** is a piece of furniture for one person to sit on. Chairs have a back, four legs, and sometimes two arms.

いすは、1人が座るための家具です。いすには背もたれ、4本の脚、場合によっては2つのひじかけがあります。

📝 furniture は「家具」、ここでの arm は「(いすの)ひじかけ」という意味。

067
bike
/ báɪk /

名 **自転車**

A **bike** is a vehicle with two wheels which you ride by pushing two pedals with your feet. Bikes are steered with handlebars.

自転車は、2つのペダルを足で踏んで乗る二輪の乗り物です。自転車はハンドルで操縦します。

📝bicycleとも言う。steerは「〈車など〉を操縦する」という意味。

068
shoe
/ ʃúː /

名 **靴**

Shoes are objects which you wear on your feet. They are often made of leather or canvas, and you wear them over socks.

靴は、足に履くものです。多くの場合、革かキャンバス地でできており、靴下の上に着用します。

📝ふつう複数形で使う。

□□□ **069**

hat

/ hǽt /

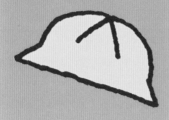

名 帽子

A **hat** is a piece of clothing which you wear on your head. Hats are worn for warmth, protection, or decoration.

帽子は、頭にかぶる衣類です。帽子は防寒、保護、または装飾のために身に着けます。

□□□ **070**

backpack

/ bǽkpæ̀k /

名 リュック

A **backpack** is a bag with two shoulder straps. Backpacks are used for carrying things on your back, often while hiking or walking.

リュックは、2本の肩ひもがついたかばんです。リュックは、よくハイキングやウォーキングの際に、ものを背負って運ぶのに使います。

✐ イギリス英語では rucksack と言う。

Scene

6

Space

宇宙

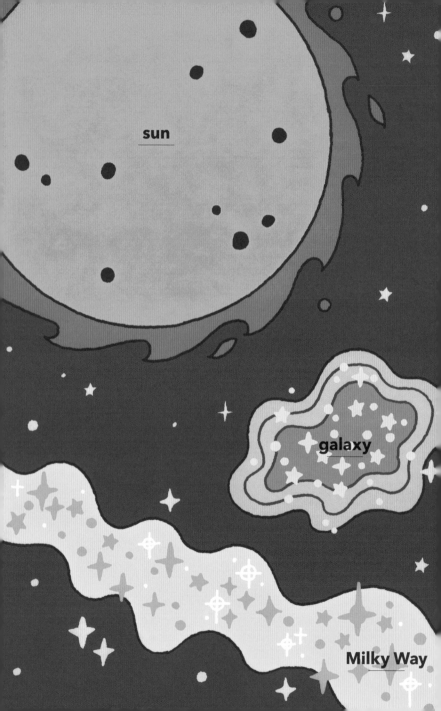

□□□ **071**

Earth

/ ə́:rθ /

名 地球

The Earth is the planet on which we live. It is the third planet from the sun.

地球は、私たちが住む惑星です。太陽から3番目の惑星です。

✎ この意味では大文字で始めることが多い。

□□□ **072**

sun

/ sʌ́n /

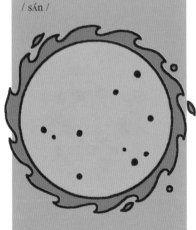

名 太陽

The sun is the star which the Earth moves around and which gives us heat and light.

太陽は、地球が周回し、私たちに熱と光をもたらしている恒星です。

21

073

moon

/ múːn /

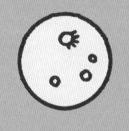

名 月

The moon is the round object which moves around the Earth every 28 days and shines at night by reflecting light from the sun.

月は、28日ごとに地球を周回し、夜に太陽からの光を反射して輝く丸い物体です。

074

star

/ stáːr /

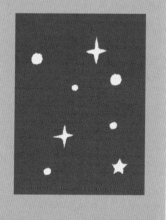

名 星、恒星

A **star** is a large ball of burning gas in space. Stars can be seen as small points of light in the sky at night.

恒星は、宇宙で燃えるガスの大きな球体です。恒星は夜空の小さな光の点として見えます。

□□□ **075**

comet

/ káːmɪt /

名 彗星

A **comet** is a bright object which moves around the sun. Comets are made up of ice and dust and have a long tail.

彗星は、太陽を周回する明るい物体です。彗星は氷とちりでできており、長い尾があります。

□□□ **076**

galaxy

/ gǽləksi /

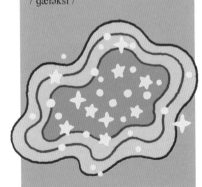

名 星雲

A **galaxy** is an extremely large group of stars and planets held together by gravity.

星雲は、重力によって結びついている、恒星と惑星の非常に大きな一団です。

✐gravity は「重力」という意味。「銀河系」は the Galaxy と言う。

□□ 077

rocket

/ rάːkət /

名 ロケット

A **rocket** is a spacecraft which is shaped like a long tube. Rockets are driven by hot gases released from engines in their rear.

ロケットは、長いチューブのような形をした宇宙船です。ロケットは後部のエンジンから放出される熱いガスによって動きます。

📝 rearは「(何かの)後部」という意味。

□□ 078

astronaut

/ ǽstrənɔ̀ːt /

名 宇宙飛行士

An **astronaut** is a person who travels into space and works in a spacecraft.

宇宙飛行士は、宇宙に行き、宇宙船で作業を行う人です。

□□□ **079**

satellite

/ sǽtəlàɪt /

名 衛星

A **satellite** is a machine sent into space which moves around the Earth or other planets, moons, etc.

衛星は、地球やほかの惑星、月などを周回する、宇宙に送られる機械です。

📝 月などのnatural satellite（衛星）と区別するためartificial satellite（人工衛星）と言うこともある。

□□□ **080**

Milky Way

/ mílki wéɪ /

名 天の川

The Milky Way is the pale band of starlight which can be seen across the night sky.

天の川は、夜空を横切って見える淡い帯状の星の光です。

📝 常に大文字で始める。

Scene

7

Body / Clothes

身体／衣服

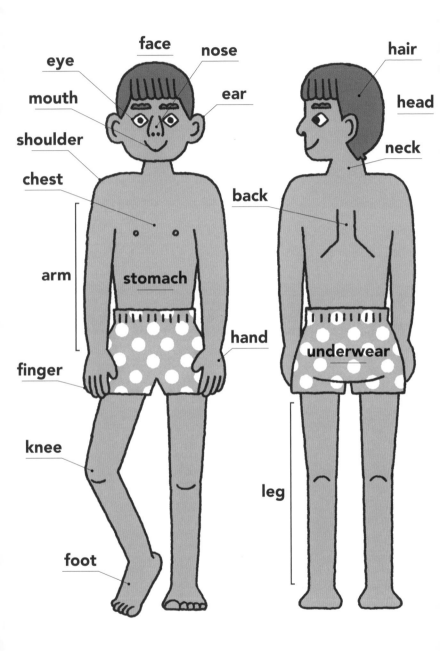

□□□ **081**

head

/ héd /

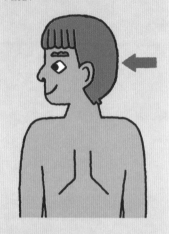

名 **頭、頭部**

Your **head** is the top part of your body, which has your brain, eyes, ears, nose, mouth, etc.

頭部は体のてっぺんにある部位で、そこに脳や目、耳、鼻、口などがあります。

✐顔を含む首から上の部分全体を指す。

□□□ **082**

hair

/ héər /

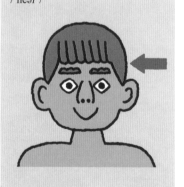

名 **髪、毛**

Your **hair** is the mass of thin threads which grow on your head and body.

髪は、頭と体に生える細い糸状のもののかたまりです。

✐体に生える「毛」全般を言う。

24

□□ 083

face

/ féɪs /

身体

名 顔

Your **face** is the front part of your head which has your eyes, nose, mouth, etc.

衣服

顔は、目、鼻、口などのある頭部の前面の部位です。

□□ 084

eye

/ áɪ /

名 目

Your **eyes** are the two parts of your face with which you see.

目は、ものを見るのに使う、顔の2つの部位です。

□□□ **085**

ear

/ íər /

名 耳

Your **ears** are the two parts of your body on either side of your head with which you hear.

耳は、音を聞くのに使う、頭部の両側にある体の2つの部位です。

□□□ **086**

nose

/ nóuz /

名 鼻

Your **nose** is the part of your face which sticks out above your mouth. You use it to smell and breathe.

鼻は、口の上に突き出ている顔の部位です。においをかいだり呼吸したりするのに使います。

✐ stick out は「突き出る」という意味。

25

087

mouth

/ máυθ /

名 口

Your **mouth** is the part of your face below your nose. You use it to eat and speak.

口は、鼻の下にある顔の部位です。食べたり話したりするのに使います。

088

neck

/ nék /

名 首

Your **neck** is the part of your body which connects your head to the rest of your body.

首は、頭部を体のその他の部分とつなぐ体の部位です。

□□□ **089**

shoulder

/ ʃóuldər /

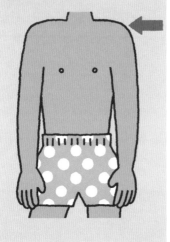

名 肩

Your **shoulders** are the parts of your body between your neck and the top of your arms.

肩は、首と腕の上部の間にある体の部位です。

□□□ **090**

chest

/ tʃést /

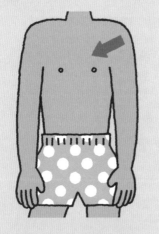

名 胸部

Your **chest** is the front part of your body between your neck and your stomach.

胸部は、首と腹の間にある体の前面の部位です。

✐「乳房」は breast と言う。

arm

/ á:rm /

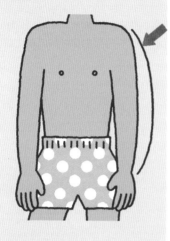

名 腕

Your **arms** are the two long parts of your body which extend from your shoulders down to your hands.

腕は、肩から手へと伸びる体の2つの長い部位です。

hand

/ hǽnd /

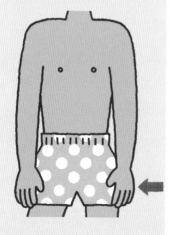

名 手

Your **hands** are the parts of your body at the end of your arms which include your fingers and thumbs.

手は、親指とその他の指を含む、腕の先端にある体の部位です。

□□□ **093**

finger

/ fíŋgər /

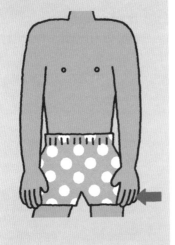

图 (手の)指

Your **fingers** are the four long thin parts at the end of each hand, not including your thumb.

指は、それぞれの手の先端にある4つの細長い部位で、親指は除きます。

🖊 ふつう親指(thumb)以外を指す。「足の指」はtoeと言う。

□□□ **094**

stomach

/ stʌ́mək /

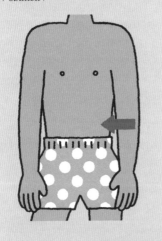

图 腹、おなか

Your **stomach** is the front part of your body just below your chest.

腹は、胸部のすぐ下の体の前面にある部位です。

🖊 「胃」という意味もある。

27

□□ **095**

back

/ bǽk /

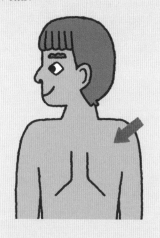

名 背中

Your **back** is the part of your body between your head and your legs which is on the opposite side of your chest.

背中は、胸部の反対側にある、頭部と脚の間の体の部位です。

□ **096**

leg

/ lég /

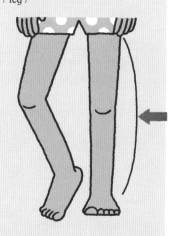

名 脚

Your **legs** are the long parts of your body which connect your feet to the rest of your body and are used to stand or walk.

脚は、足を体のその他の部分とつなぐ体の長い部位で、立ったり歩いたりするのに使います。

□□□ **097**

knee

/ níː /

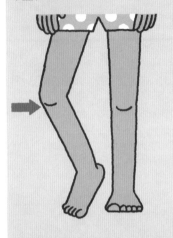

图 ひざ

Your **knee** is the joint which bends in the middle of your legs.

ひざは、脚の真ん中で曲がる関節です。

□□□ **098**

foot

/ fút /

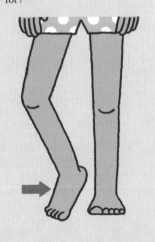

图 足

Your **feet** are the parts of your body at the end of your legs, on which you stand.

足は、立つときに踏みしめる、脚の先端にある体の部位です。

✐ 複数形は feet / fíːt /。

28

099

underwear

/ ʌ́ndərwèər /

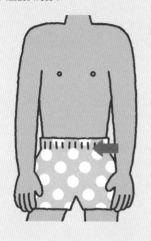

名 **下着**

Underwear is clothing which you wear next to your body under your other clothes.

下着は体にじかに身につける衣類で、ほかの服の下に着ます。

100

shirt

/ ʃə́ːrt /

名 **シャツ**

A **shirt** is a piece of clothing which you wear on the upper part of your body. It is usually fastened at the front with buttons.

シャツは、上半身に着る服です。ふつう前側をボタンで留めます。

□□□ **101**

pants

/ pǽnts /

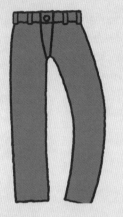

名 ズボン

Pants are a piece of clothing which covers your lower body and is divided into two separate parts for each leg.

ズボンは下半身を覆う服で、それぞれの脚用に2つの別々の部分に分かれています。

常に複数形で使う。イギリス英語では trousers と言う。

□□□ **102**

sweater

/ swétər /

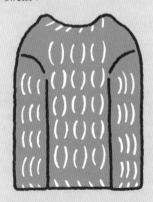

名 セーター

A **sweater** is a warm knitted piece of clothing with long sleeves which you wear on the upper part of your body.

セーターは、上半身に着る、編んで作った暖かい長袖の服です。

□□ **103**

jacket

/ ʤǽkɪt /

名 ジャケット

A **jacket** is a short coat with long sleeves.

ジャケットは、長袖の短いコートです。

□□ **104**

sock

/ sάːk /

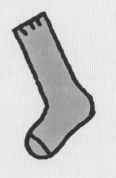

名 靴下

Socks are soft pieces of clothing which cover your foot, and often your ankle and the lower part of your leg. They are worn inside shoes.

靴下は、足、そしてしばしば足首と脚の下の部分を覆う柔らかい衣類です。靴の内側に履きます。

✐ふつう複数形で使う。

□□□ **105**

tie
/ táɪ /

名 **ネクタイ**

A **tie** is a long narrow piece of cloth worn mostly by men. It is worn around the neck under a shirt collar and tied with a knot in front.

ネクタイは、主に男性が着用する細長い布です。シャツの襟の内側で首に巻き、前で結び目を作ります。

✑necktie はやや古い語。

□□□ **106**

belt
/ bélt /

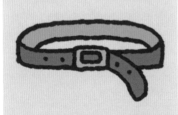

名 **ベルト**

A **belt** is a band of leather or cloth which you wear around your waist to hold up your clothes or for decoration.

ベルトは、衣服を支えるため、あるいは装飾のために腰に巻く、革または布の帯です。

✑hold up は「〜を支える」という意味。

107

dress

/ drés /

名 ワンピース

A **dress** is a piece of clothing for a woman or girl which covers the body and part of the legs.

ワンピースは、体と脚の一部を覆う、女性や女の子のための服です。

✐ one piece とは言わない。

108

skirt

/ skə́:rt /

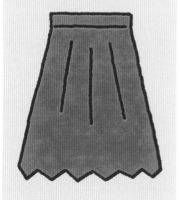

名 スカート

A **skirt** is a piece of clothing for a woman or girl which hangs down from the waist.

スカートは、腰から下げるようにして着る、女性や女の子のための服です。

身体

衣服

□□□ **109**

necklace

/ nékləs /

名 ネックレス

A **necklace** is a piece of jewelry consisting of a chain, string of beads, etc. which you wear around your neck.

ネックレスは鎖やつなげたビーズなどからなる宝飾品で、首の周りに着けます。

✐jewelryは「宝飾品類」、consist ofは「〜からなる」という意味。

□□□ **110**

glasses

/ glǽsɪz /

名 眼鏡

Glasses are two lenses in a frame, which you wear in front of your eyes in order to see clearly.

眼鏡はフレームに2つのレンズがはまったもので、ものをはっきり見るために目の前に着けます。

✐この意味では常に複数形で使う。

Scene

8

Living room

居間

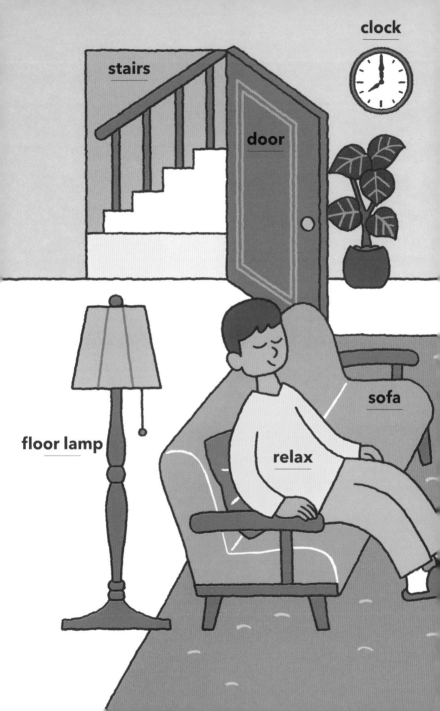

painting

bookcase

TV

cushion

table

candle

cup

rug

□□□ **111**

sofa

/ sóufə /

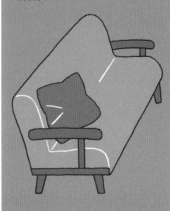

名 ソファー

A **sofa** is a long and comfortable seat with a back and arms. It is wide enough for two or three people to sit on.

ソファーは、背もたれとひじかけのある長くて快適ないすです。 2、3人座れるくらいの幅があります。

✐couchとも言う。

□□□ **112**

TV

/ tì:ví: /

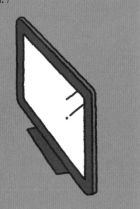

名 テレビ

A **TV** is a piece of electrical equipment with a screen on the front, on which you can watch programs with moving pictures and sounds.

テレビは、前面に画面があり、動画や音声のある番組を見ることのできる電気機器です。

✐televisionとも言う。

32

113

cushion

/ kúʃən /

名 クッション

A **cushion** is a cloth bag filled with something soft which you put on a seat to make it more comfortable.

クッションは、座面の座り心地をよりよくするために置く、柔らかいものを詰めた布製の袋です。

114

stairs

/ stéərz /

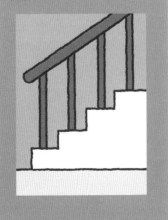

名 階段

Stairs are a set of steps which lead up and down to different levels, such as in a building.

階段は、建物の中などで上や下の階に行くための一連の踏み段です。

✐ この意味ではふつう複数形で使う。

※イラストを見ながら、英語を英語で理解しよう

□□□ **115**

table

/ téɪbl /

名 テーブル

A **table** is a piece of furniture with a flat top which you put things on, supported by one or more legs.

テーブルはものを置く平らな天板のある家具で、1本または複数の脚で支えられています。

□□□ **116**

door

/ dɔ́ːr /

名 ドア

A **door** is a large flat piece of wood, glass, metal, etc. which you move when you go into or out of a building, room, vehicle, etc.

ドアは木やガラス、金属などでできた大きく平らなもので、建物、部屋、乗り物などに出入りするときに動かします。

33

117

rug

/ rʌ́g /

名 ラグ

A **rug** is a piece of thick material which covers part of a floor and is used for warmth or as a decoration.

ラグは床の一部を覆う厚い生地で、暖を取るためや装飾として使います。

✐ carpet（カーペット、じゅうたん）はより広い面を覆うものを指す。

118

bookcase

/ bʊ́kkèɪs /

名 本棚

A **bookcase** is a piece of furniture with shelves for putting books on.

本棚は、本をのせる棚のある家具です。

□□□ **119**

floor lamp

/ flɔ́ːr lǽmp /

名 フロアランプ

A **floor lamp** is a tall electric light which stands on the floor. It consists of a tall pole with a lampshade at the top.

フロアランプは、床に立つ背の高い電灯です。上部にランプシェードがある高いポールでできています。

□□□ **120**

clock

/ klɑ́ːk /

名 時計

A **clock** is a device which tells you what time it is. Clocks are often hung on walls or shown on digital screens.

時計は、時刻を伝えるための装置です。時計はしばしば壁にかけられたり、デジタル画面に表示されたりします。

121

painting

/ péintiŋ /

名 絵画

A **painting** is a picture which someone has painted. It is made by putting paint on a canvas, board, etc.

絵画は、人が描いた絵です。カンバスや板などに絵の具を塗って作ります。

✐「線画」はdrawingと言う。

122

candle

/ kǽndl /

名 ろうそく

A **candle** is a round stick of wax with a piece of string through the middle which you burn to make light.

ろうそくは真ん中に1本のひもが通った丸いろうの棒で、燃やして光を作ります。

✐「(ろうそくの)芯」はwickと言う。

□□□ **123**

cup
/ kʌ́p /

名 カップ

A **cup** is a small round container, often with a handle. It is used for drinking drinks, such as tea, coffee, etc.

カップは小さな丸い容器で、しばしば持ち手がついています。紅茶やコーヒーなどの飲み物を飲むのに使います。

□□□ **124**

relax
/ rɪlǽks /

動 くつろぐ

When you **relax**, you rest and feel more calm and less worried or nervous.

リラックスするとき、人は休息し、落ち着きが増して心配や緊張が和らぎます。

he japan times *alpha*

「The Japan Times Alpha」は
ジャパンタイムズが発行する英語
学習者のための週刊紙です。
その週に起きた重要なニュース、
世界中のトレンドなどの英文記事を
無理なく読み切れるボリュームで掲
載。和訳・解説付きなので、辞書
をひく手間を省いて効率的に英語表
現をインプットし、日本や世界の「今」
を語る英語力をつけるのに最適です。

● 毎週金曜日発行　● タブロイド判　24頁(標準)

下記からの
お申込みで

Scene

9

Bedroom / Study

寝室／書斎

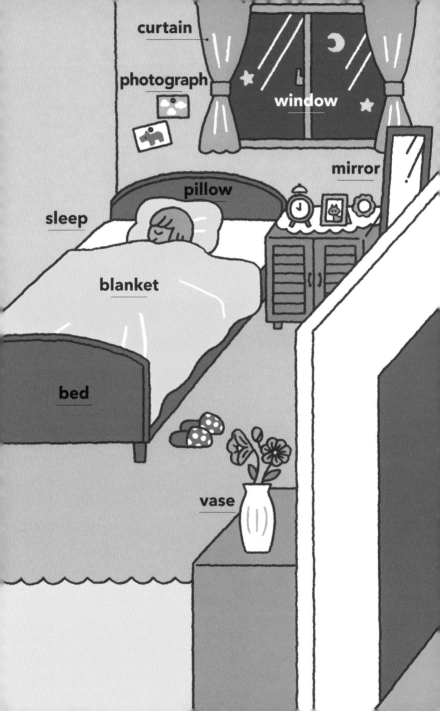

□□□ **125**

window

/ wíndou /

名 窓

A **window** is an opening in a wall, door, etc. which allows light, air, etc. to pass through it. It usually has glass in it.

窓は壁やドアなどの開口部で、光や空気などが通り抜けられるようになっています。ふつうガラスがはめられています。

□□□ **126**

curtain

/ kə́:rtn /

名 カーテン

Curtains are large pieces of cloth which you hang to cover a window.

カーテンは、窓を覆うためにつるす大きな布です。

🖉drape とも言う。

36

□□ **127**

bed

/ béd /

名 ベッド

A **bed** is a large, rectangular piece of furniture which you sleep on.

ベッドは大きな長方形の家具で、その上で眠ります。

✐ rectangular は「長方形の」という意味。

□□ **128**

blanket

/ blǽŋkət /

名 毛布

A **blanket** is a large cover, often made of wool, which you use on a bed to keep you warm.

毛布は大きなカバーで、しばしばウールでできており、ベッドで体を温かく保つのに使います。

□□□ **129**

pillow

/ píloʊ /

名 枕

A **pillow** is a rectangular cloth bag filled with soft material which you rest your head on when you are in bed.

枕は柔らかい素材を詰めた長方形の布製の袋で、ベッドにいるとき頭をのせます。

□□□ **130**

mirror

/ mírər /

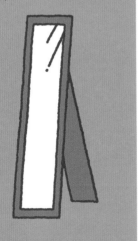

名 鏡

A **mirror** is a piece of special flat glass which reflects images so that you can see yourself or what is behind you when you look in it.

鏡は像を反射する特殊な板ガラスで、それをのぞくと自分自身や自分の背後にあるものが見えるようになっています。

37

131

photograph

/ fóutəgrὲf /

名 写真

A **photograph** is a picture of something which you make by using a camera.

写真は、カメラを使って作る、何かの像です。

📝 photo、picture とも言う。

132

vase

/ véɪs /

名 花びん

A **vase** is a container which is used for holding cut flowers or as an ornament.

花びんは、切り花を入れるのに使ったり、装飾として使ったりする容器です。

103

□□□ **133**

sleep

/ slíːp /

動 眠る

When you **sleep**, you rest your mind and body by lying down with your eyes closed, usually at night.

眠るとき、人はふつう夜に目を閉じて横になり、心と体を休ませます。

✎sleep-slept-slept と活用する。

□□□ **134**

desk

/ désk /

名 机

A **desk** is a piece of furniture like a table, often with drawers, where you sit to read, write, work, etc.

机はテーブルに似た家具で、しばしば引き出しがついており、そこで座ってものを読んだり、書いたり、仕事をしたりします。

38

□□ **135**

pencil

/ pénsl /

图 えんぴつ

A **pencil** is an instrument used for writing and drawing. It is often wooden and has a black or colored part in the middle.

えんぴつは、書いたり線画を描いたりするのに使う道具です。しばしば木製で、真ん中に黒または色のついた部分があります。

□□ **136**

eraser

/ ɪréɪsər /

图 消しゴム

An **eraser** is a small piece of rubber or a similar substance, used for removing something you have written or drawn with a pencil.

消しゴムは、えんぴつで書いたり線画を描いたりしたものを消すのに使う、ゴムまたはそれに似た素材の小さな断片です。

✍ substanceは「物質」という意味。

□□□ **137**

notebook

/ nóʊtbùk /

名 ノート

A **notebook** is a book of blank pages, usually with lines, which is used for writing notes.

ノートは何も書かれていないページででき た本で、ふつう罫線があり、メモを書くため に使います。

□□□ **138**

book

/ búk /

名 本

A **book** is a set of printed pages which are held together in a cover so that you can read them.

本は、読むことができるようにカバーでとじら れた、ひとまとまりの印刷されたページです。

139
dictionary

/ díkʃənèri /

名 辞書

A **dictionary** is a reference book which gives information about words and their meanings, uses, pronunciations, etc.

辞書は、語とその意味、使いかた、発音などに関する情報を提供する参考図書です。

140
calendar

/ kǽləndər /

名 カレンダー

A **calendar** is a printed table showing all the days, weeks, and months of a particular year, which you usually hang on a wall.

カレンダーは、特定の年のすべての日、週、月を示す印刷された表で、ふつう壁にかけられます。

📝ここでのtableは「表」という意味。

40

□□□ **141**

scissors

/ sízərz /

名 はさみ

Scissors are a tool used for cutting things, such as paper, cloth, and hair. It has two sharp blades with handles, joined together in the middle.

はさみは、紙や布、髪などを切るのに使う道具です。2枚の鋭利な刃と持ち手があり、中央で結合されています。

✐ この意味では常に複数形で使う。blade は「刃」という意味。

□□□ **142**

read

/ ríːd /

動 ～を読む

When you **read** something such as a book, you look at the words which are written there and understand their meaning.

本などを読むとき、人はそこに書かれている言葉を見て、その意味を理解します。

✐ read-read-read と活用する。過去形と過去分詞形の発音は / réd /。

Scene

10

Kitchen

キッチン

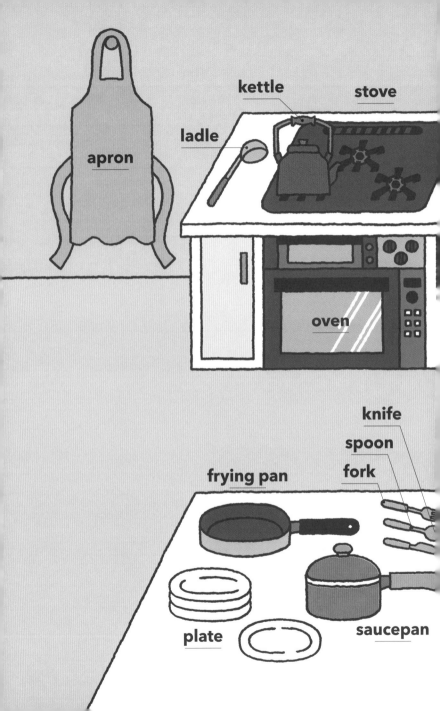

kettle

stove

ladle

apron

oven

knife

spoon

fork

frying pan

plate

saucepan

□□□ **143**

saucepan

/ sɔ́ːspæ̀n /

名 片手なべ

A **saucepan** is a deep, round metal pot with a lid and a long handle, which is used for cooking food over heat.

片手なべは、ふたと長い柄のついた深くて丸い金属製のなべで、火にかけて食べ物を調理するのに使います。

□□□ **144**

frying pan

/ frάiŋ pæ̀n /

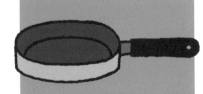

名 フライパン

A **frying pan** is a shallow metal pot with a long handle, which is used for frying food.

フライパンは長い柄のついた浅い金属製のなべで、食べ物をいためるのに使います。

41

145

stove

/ stóuv /

名 コンロ

A **stove** is a piece of kitchen equipment on which you cook food in pots and pans.

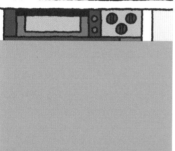

コンロは、深なべや平なべをのせて調理するための台所設備です。

146

oven

/ ʌ́vn /

名 オーブン

An **oven** is a large piece of kitchen equipment which is like a box with a door. You bake or roast food inside it.

オーブンは、ドアのついた箱のような大型の台所設備です。中に食べ物を入れ、焼いたりローストしたりします。

□□□ **147**

plate

/ pléɪt /

名 皿、平皿

A **plate** is a flat and usually round dish which is used to put food on.

平皿は、食べ物をのせるのに使う、平らでふつう円形の皿です。

✐「(大きい)盛り皿」はdishと言う。

□□□ **148**

fork

/ fɔ́ːrk /

名 フォーク

A **fork** is a metal or plastic tool used for picking up and eating food. It has a handle and three or four sharp points.

フォークは、食べ物を取って食べるのに使う、金属またはプラスチック製の道具です。取っ手と3つか4つの鋭い先端があります。

42

149

spoon

/ spúːn /

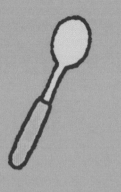

名 スプーン

A **spoon** is a metal or plastic tool used for mixing, serving, and eating food. It has a handle and a shallow bowl.

スプーンは、食べ物を混ぜたり、よそったり、食べたりするのに使う、金属またはプラスチック製の道具です。取っ手と浅いボウル状の部分があります。

150

knife

/ náɪf /

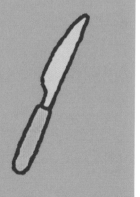

名 ナイフ、包丁

A **knife** is a tool used for cutting food. It usually has a sharp metal blade and a handle.

ナイフは、食べ物を切るのに使う道具です。ふつう鋭利な金属の刃と取っ手があります。

□□□ **151**

apron

/ éɪprən /

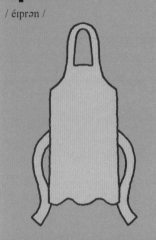

名 エプロン

An **apron** is a piece of clothing which is worn over the front of the body over clothes to keep them from getting dirty.

エプロンは、服が汚れるのを防ぐために、体の前面を覆うように服の上に着用する衣類です。

□□□ **152**

kettle

/ kétl /

名 やかん

A **kettle** is a container used for boiling and pouring water. It has a lid, a handle, and a spout.

やかんは、お湯を沸かして注ぐのに使う容器です。ふた、取っ手、注ぎ口がついています。

43

153

ladle

/ léɪdl /

名 おたま

A **ladle** is a large, round, deep spoon with a long handle, used for serving soup, stew, etc.

おたまは長い柄のついた大きくて丸く深いスプーンで、スープやシチューなどをよそうのに使います。

154

bottle

/ bάːtl /

名 びん

A **bottle** is a glass or plastic container for liquids. Bottles are usually round and have a narrow top.

びんは、ガラスまたはプラスチック製の液体用の容器です。びんはふつう丸く、上部が細くなっています。

□□□ **155**

sink

/ síŋk /

图 流し

A **sink** is a large open container usually attached to a wall. It is connected to pipes which bring water and carry it away.

流しは、ふつう壁に取りつけられた大きなふたのない容器です。水を引いたり排出したりする管につながっています。

✐ ここでのopenは「ふたがない」という意味。

□□□ **156**

cut

/ kʌ́t /

動 〜を切る

When you **cut** something, you divide it into two or more pieces with a knife, scissors, etc.

ものを切るとき、人はナイフ、はさみなどでそれを2つ以上に分けます。

✐ cut-cut-cutと活用する。

157

salt

/ sɔ́ːlt /

名 塩

Salt is a white substance which is added to food before or after cooking to make it taste better or to preserve it.

塩は、食べ物の味をよくしたり食べ物を保存したりするために、調理の前後に食べ物に加える白い物質です。

🖉 preserve は「〜を保存する」という意味。

158

sugar

/ ʃúɡər /

名 砂糖

Sugar is a sweet substance usually in the form of white or brown crystals or white powder, which is used to make food and drinks sweet.

砂糖は、ふつう白や茶色の結晶、または白い粉末状の甘い物質で、食べ物や飲み物を甘くするのに使います。

□□□ **159**

pepper

/ pépər /

图 コショウ

Pepper is a spice made from dried berries, which is used to give a hot flavor to food.

コショウは干した実から作られるスパイスで、食べ物に辛い風味をつけるのに使います。

□□□ **160**

oil

/ ɔ́ɪl /

图 油

Oil is a smooth, thick liquid made from plants or animals, which is often used in cooking.

油は植物や動物から作られる滑らかな濃い液体で、よく料理に使います。

✐ ここでのthickは「濃い、濃厚な」という意味。

Scene
11

Garden

庭

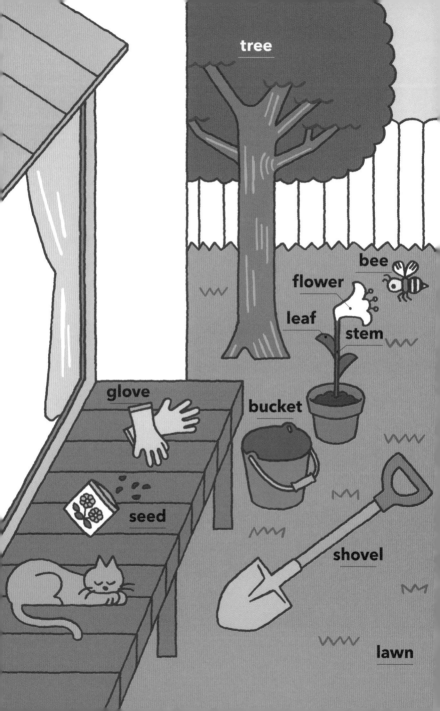

butterfly

water

flowerbed

snail

□□□ **161**

flowerbed

/ fláʊərbèd /

名 花壇

A **flowerbed** is an area of ground in a garden or park where flowers are grown.

花壇は、花が育てられる、庭や公園の区画です。

□□□ **162**

bucket

/ bʌ́kət /

名 バケツ

A **bucket** is an open container with a handle which is used to hold and carry things, especially liquids.

バケツは持ち手のあるふたのない容器で、特に液体などのものを入れて運ぶために使います。

46

163

flower

/ fláʊər /

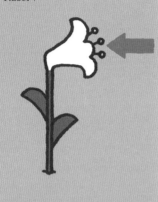

名 花

A **flower** is the part of a plant from which the seed or fruit develops. Flowers are often brightly colored and have a pleasant smell.

花は、そこから種や実のできる植物の部位です。花はしばしば色が鮮やかで、よい香りがします。

📝「花の咲く植物」もflowerと言う。

164

seed

/ síːd /

名 種

A **seed** is a small, hard object produced by a plant, from which a new plant of the same kind grows.

種は植物によって生み出される小さく硬い物体で、そこから同じ種類の新しい植物が成長します。

□□□ **165**

leaf

/ líːf /

名 葉

The **leaves** of a tree or plant are the flat, thin, and usually green parts which grow on a branch or stem.

木や植物の葉は、平らで薄くふつう緑色の部位で、枝や茎から生えます。

□□□ **166**

stem

/ stém /

名 茎

The **stem** of a plant is the long, thin, and upright part above the ground on which the flowers and leaves grow.

植物の茎は、地上に出ている細長く直立した部位で、そこから花と葉が生えます。

✐「(ワイングラスなどの)脚」も stem と言う。

47

167

water

/ wɔ́ːtər /

動 〜に水をやる

When you **water** plants, you pour water on them.

植物に水をやるとき、人はそれらに水を注ぎます。

168

bee

/ bíː /

名 ミツバチ

A **bee** is a flying insect which has a black-and-yellow striped body. Bees can sting. They live in social groups and make honey.

ミツバチは、黒と黄色のしま模様の体を持つ飛ぶ昆虫です。ミツバチは刺すことがあります。群れを成して生活し、蜂蜜を作ります。

□□□ **169**

butterfly

/ bʌ́tərflàɪ /

名 チョウ

A **butterfly** is a flying insect which has a thin body and brightly-colored wings. Butterflies are most active during the day.

チョウは、細い体と色鮮やかな羽を持つ飛ぶ昆虫です。チョウは日中が最も活動的です。

□□□ **170**

glove

/ ɡlʌ́v /

名 手袋

Gloves are pieces of clothing which you wear on your hands in order to protect them or keep them warm.

手袋は手に着用する衣類で、手を保護したり温かく保ったりするのに使います。

✐ ふつう複数形で使う。

171

shovel

/ ʃʌ́vl /

名 シャベル

A **shovel** is a tool with a rounded blade and a long handle. Shovels are used for lifting and moving soil, snow, sand, etc.

シャベルは、丸みをつけた刃と長い柄のある道具です。シャベルは土や雪、砂などを持ち上げたり移動したりするのに使います。

172

snail

/ snéɪl /

名 カタツムリ

A **snail** is a small animal with a soft body and a spiral shell on its back. Snails move very slowly.

カタツムリは、柔らかい体を持ち、背中にらせん状の殻をのせた小動物です。カタツムリはとてもゆっくりと動きます。

🖉 spiral は「らせん状の」という意味。

□□□ **173**

tree

/ tríː /

名 木

A **tree** is a large tall plant which has a hard trunk, branches, and leaves. Trees live for a long time.

木は大きな背の高い植物で、硬い幹、枝、葉があります。木は長生きします。

□□□ **174**

lawn

/ lɔːn /

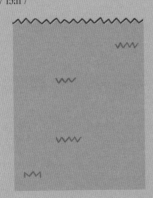

名 芝生

A **lawn** is an area of grass, especially around a house or in a garden or park, which is cut regularly to keep it short.

芝生は特に家の周り、または庭や公園にある草の区画で、短くしておくために定期的に刈られます。

Scene

12

City

街

helicopter

bridge

amusement park

street

CINEMA

museum

bus stop

traffic light

movie theater

bus

hotel

intersection

crosswalk

railroad crossing

walk

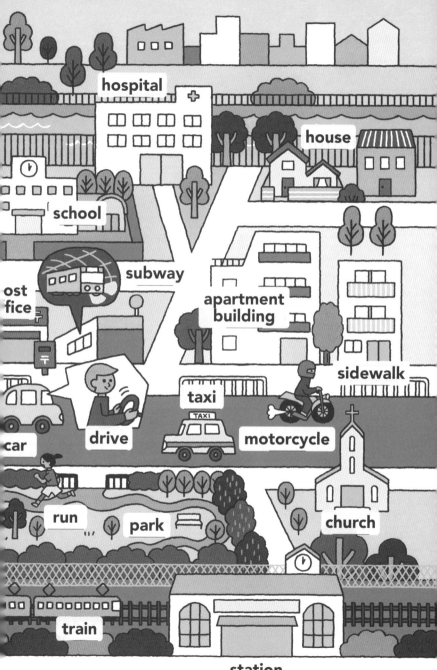

□□□ 175

street

/ stríːt /

名 通り

A **street** is a public road in a city or town which has houses or other buildings on one or both sides.

通りは都市や町の公道で、片側または両側に家やその他の建物があります。

□□□ 176

intersection

/ ìntərsékʃən /

名 交差点

An **intersection** is a place where two or more things, especially streets, meet or cross each other.

交差点は、2つ以上のもの、特に通りが合流したり交差したりする場所です。

50

177

traffic light

/ trǽfɪk làɪt /

名 信号機

Traffic lights are a set of red, green, and yellow lights to control traffic, usually at a point where two or more roads meet.

信号機は赤、青、黄色で1セットの信号灯で、ふつう2つ以上の道路が合流する地点で交通を制御します。

178

sidewalk

/ sáɪdwɔ̀ːk /

名 歩道

A **sidewalk** is a path with a hard surface at the side of a street for people to walk on.

歩道は、人が歩くための、通りの脇の舗装された通路です。

□□□ **179**

crosswalk

/ krɔ́(:)swɔ̀:k /

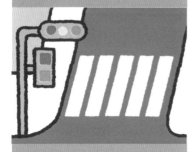

名 **横断歩道**

A **crosswalk** is a marked place on a road where vehicles must stop to let people walk across.

横断歩道は道路上に印のついた場所で、そこでは人が横断できるように車両は停止しなければなりません。

□□□ **180**

park

/ páːrk /

名 **公園**

A **park** is an open public area with grass and trees, usually in a town, where people can walk, relax, play, etc.

公園は草や木のある開放された公共の区域で、ふつう町の中にあり、人が散歩したりくつろいだり、遊んだりすることができます。

✐ここでのopenは「開放された」という意味。

51

181

school

/ skúːl /

名 学校

A **school** is a place where children go to be educated.

学校は、子どもたちが教育を受けに行く場所です。

182

post office

/ póʊst àːfəs /

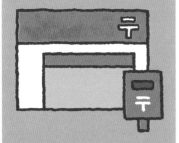

名 郵便局

A **post office** is a place where you can buy stamps, send letters and parcels, etc.

郵便局は、切手を買ったり、手紙や小包を送ったりすることのできる場所です。

museum

/ mjú(ː)zíːəm /

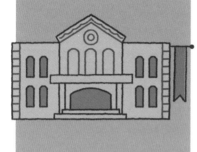

名 博物館、美術館

A **museum** is a building where interesting and valuable things, such as works of art or historical items, are collected and displayed to the public.

博物館（美術館）は、芸術作品や歴史的事物といった、興味深く価値のあるものを集めて一般向けに展示する建物です。

✐ display は「〜を展示する」という意味。

amusement park

/ əmjúːzmənt pàːrk /

名 遊園地

An **amusement park** is a large place with many special machines which you can ride on for entertainment, such as roller coasters and Ferris wheels.

遊園地は、ジェットコースターや観覧車など、娯楽目的で乗ることができるたくさんの特別な機械がある広い場所です。

52

185

movie theater

/ múːvi θíːətər /

名 映画館

A **movie theater** is a building where you go to watch films for entertainment.

映画館は、娯楽のために映画を見に行く建物です。

⬛ イギリス英語では cinema と言う。

186

church

/ tʃə́ːrtʃ /

名 教会

A **church** is a building which Christians use for religious activities.

教会は、キリスト教徒が宗教活動のために使う建物です。

139

□□□ **187**

hotel

/ houtél /

名 ホテル

A **hotel** is a building where you pay to stay, especially when you are traveling. Hotels often provide meals or other services for guests.

ホテルは、特に旅行中にお金を払って滞在する建物です。多くの場合、ホテルは客に食事やその他のサービスを提供します。

□□□ **188**

house

/ háus /

名 家

A **house** is a building to live in. It is usually used by one family.

家は、住むための建物です。ふつう1つの家族が使います。

✐複数形housesは / háuzɪz / と発音する。

53

189

apartment building

/ əpáːrtmənt bìldɪŋ /

名 マンション、アパート

An **apartment building** is a large building which has several apartments.

マンション（アパート）は、複数の住居区画がある大きな建物です。

📝apartmentは、共同住宅の建物のうちの「1家族用の居住部分」を指す。

190

hospital

/ háːspɪtl /

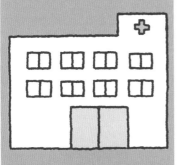

名 病院

A **hospital** is a large building where sick or injured people are given medical treatment and taken care of by doctors and nurses.

病院は、病気やけがをした人が医師と看護師から治療と手当てを受ける大きな建物です。

□□□ **191**

bridge

/ bríʤ /

名 橋

A **bridge** is a structure which is built over a river, road, etc. so that people or vehicles can cross from one side to the other.

橋は川や道路などに架かる建造物で、人や車両が片側から反対側へ渡ることができるようになっています。

□□□ **192**

helicopter

/ héləkà:ptər /

名 ヘリコプター

A **helicopter** is a type of aircraft with large blades on top which turn around very fast. It can take off and land vertically and stay in one place in the air.

ヘリコプターは、高速で回転する大きな翼が上部にあるタイプの航空機です。垂直に離着陸し、空中で一か所にとどまることができます。

✐ここでのblade は「翼」、verticallyは「垂直に」という意味。

54

193
train
/ tréɪn /

名 列車

A **train** is a group of railroad cars connected to each other and usually to an engine. It takes people and goods from one place to another.

列車は、互いに連結され、ふつう機関車に接続されている一連の鉄道車両です。人やものをある場所から別の場所へと運びます。

194
station
/ stéɪʃən /

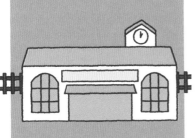

名 駅

A **station** is a building or place where trains stop so that people can get on and off.

駅は、人が乗り降りできるように列車が停止する建物や場所です。

143

□□□ **195**

railroad crossing

/ réɪlroʊd krɔ̀(ː)sɪŋ /

名 踏切

A **railroad crossing** is a place where a road crosses a railroad track at the same level.

踏切は、道路が同じ高さで線路と交差する場所です。

✐「遮断機」は crossing gate と言う。

□□□ **196**

car

/ káːr /

名 車

A **car** is a road vehicle with four wheels and an engine. It can carry a small number of people.

車は、4つの車輪とエンジンを備えた道路車両です。少数の人を運ぶことができます。

✐「(鉄道)車両」という意味もある。

197

bus

/ bʌ́s /

名 バス

A **bus** is a large road vehicle, especially one which you pay to travel on and which travels along a fixed route and stops regularly.

バスは大型の道路車両で、特に移動するためにお金を払って乗るもの、決まった路線に沿って運行し、定期的に停車するものを指します。

198

bus stop

/ bʌ́s stɑ̀:p /

名 バス停

A **bus stop** is a place at the side of a road, marked with a sign, where buses stop so that people can get on and off.

バス停は標識のある道路脇の場所で、人が乗り降りできるようにバスはそこで停車します。

□□□ **199**

motorcycle

/ móʊtərsàɪkl /

名 オートバイ

A **motorcycle** is a road vehicle with two wheels driven by an engine.

オートバイは、エンジンで動く二輪の道路車両です。

✐イギリス英語では motorbike とも言う。

□□□ **200**

taxi

/ tǽksi /

名 タクシー

A **taxi** is a car with a driver who you pay to take you somewhere based on the distance traveled.

タクシーは運転手つきの車で、その運転手に運んでもらうために移動距離に応じてお金を支払います。

201

subway

/ sʌ́bwèɪ /

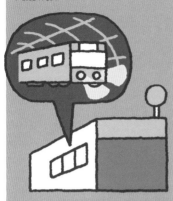

名 地下鉄

A **subway** is an underground train system in a big city.

地下鉄は、大都市の地下の鉄道システムです。

✅イギリス英語ではundergroundと言う。

202

drive

/ dráɪv /

動 ～を運転する

When you **drive** a vehicle, you control it so that it moves somewhere.

車両を運転するとき、人はそれを操作してどこかに移動させます。

✅drive-drove-drivenと活用する。

□□□ **203**

walk

/ wɔ́:k /

動 歩く

When you **walk**, you move forward by putting one foot in front of the other in a regular way and at a speed slower than running.

歩くとき、人は規則的に、走るよりも遅い速度で、一方の足をもう一方の足の前に出すことによって、前方に移動します。

✐「歩行者」はpedestrianと言う。

□□□ **204**

run

/ rʌ́n /

動 走る

When you **run**, you move with your legs at a speed faster than walking.

走るとき、人は歩くよりも速い速度で脚で移動します。

✐run-ran-runと活用する。

Scene

13

Grocery store

スーパーマーケット

□□□ **205**

carrot

/ kǽrət /

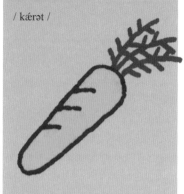

名 ニンジン

A **carrot** is a long pointed orange root of a plant. It is eaten as a vegetable.

ニンジンは、長く先のとがったオレンジ色の植物の根です。野菜として食べます。

□□□ **206**

tomato

/ təméɪtoʊ /

名 トマト

A **tomato** is a red, round, juicy fruit. It is eaten raw or cooked as a vegetable. It is often used in salads, sauces, etc.

トマトは、赤くて丸い水分の多い果実です。野菜として、生でまたは火を通して食べます。よくサラダやソースなどに使います。

58

207

onion

/ ánjən /

名 タマネギ

An **onion** is a round bulb with many layers inside. It has a strong taste and smell and is used in cooking.

タマネギは、内側に多くの層のある丸い球根です。味と香りが強く、料理に使います。

ここでのbulbは「球根」という意味。

208

cucumber

/ kjúːkλmbər /

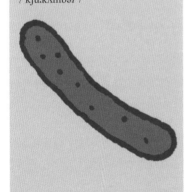

名 キュウリ

A **cucumber** is a long thin vegetable with dark green skin and light green flesh. It is often used for salads or to make pickles.

キュウリは、濃い緑色の皮と薄緑色の果肉を持つ細長い野菜です。よくサラダやピクルスに使います。

fleshは「果肉」という意味。

□□□ **209**

pumpkin

/ pʌ́mpkɪn /

名 カボチャ

A **pumpkin** is a large round vegetable with a thick orange skin and large seeds. It is used as food and sometimes as a decoration.

カボチャは、厚いオレンジ色の皮と大きな種を持つ、大きくて丸い野菜です。食用として、時に装飾として使います。

📝 濃い緑色の皮のカボチャはsquashと言う。

□□□ **210**

eggplant

/ éɡplæ̀nt /

名 ナス

An **eggplant** is an egg-shaped vegetable with shiny dark purple skin. It is soft and white inside.

ナスは、光沢のある濃い紫色の皮を持つ卵形の野菜です。内側は柔らかくて白いです。

📝 イギリス英語ではaubergineと言う。

59

211

garlic

/ gáːrlɪk /

名 ニンニク

Garlic is a vegetable like a small onion with a very strong taste and smell. It is used in cooking to add a pleasant flavor to food.

ニンニクは小さな玉ねぎのような野菜で、味と香りがとても強いです。料理で食べ物によい風味を加えるのに使います。

212

ginger

/ ʤínʤər /

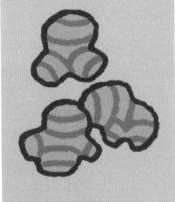

名 ショウガ

Ginger is the root of a tropical plant with a very strong taste. It is used in cooking as a spice.

ショウガは、とても強い風味のある熱帯植物の根です。料理でスパイスとして使います。

□□□ **213**

lettuce

/ léṭəs /

图 レタス

Lettuce is a large round vegetable with thin green leaves which you eat raw, especially in salad.

レタスは薄くて緑色の葉を持つ大きな丸い野菜で、特にサラダに入れて生で食べます。

□□□ **214**

potato

/ pətéɪṭoʊ /

图 ジャガイモ

A **potato** is a round vegetable which grows underground. Potatoes are white inside and brown or yellow outside.

ジャガイモは、地中で育つ丸い野菜です。ジャガイモの内側は白く、外側は茶色か黄色です。

60

215

mushroom

/ mʌ́ʃruːm /

名 キノコ

Mushrooms are fungi with short stems and round tops. They look like umbrellas. Some of them can be eaten.

キノコは、短い茎と丸い上部を持つ菌類です。傘のような外見です。食べられるものもあります。

🖉 fungus（複数形はfungi）は「菌類」という意味。

216

apple

/ ǽpl /

名 リンゴ

An **apple** is a hard, round fruit with juicy white flesh and usually red or green skin.

リンゴは硬くて丸い果実で、果肉は白くて水分が多く、皮はふつう赤または緑色です。

※イラストを見ながら、英語を英語で理解しよう

☐☐☐ **217**

lemon

/ lémən /

名 レモン

A **lemon** is a small oval citrus fruit with hard yellow skin and a very sour taste.

レモンは小さな卵形のかんきつ系の果物で、硬くて黄色い皮と強い酸味を持っています。

☐☐☐ **218**

pineapple

/ páinæpl /

名 パイナップル

A **pineapple** is a large tropical fruit with thick rough skin and stiff leaves on top. It has yellow, sweet, juicy flesh.

パイナップルは大きな熱帯の果物で、皮は厚くてごつごつしており、てっぺんには硬い葉がついています。果肉は黄色で甘く、水分を多く含んでいます。

61

219
grape
/ gréɪp /

名 ブドウ

Grapes are a small green or dark purple round fruit. They grow in bunches and can be eaten raw, used to make wine, or dried.

ブドウは、小さくて緑色または濃い紫色の丸い果実です。房状に成長し、生で食べることも、ワインを作るのに使うことも、干すこともできます。

📝 単数形は「1粒のブドウ」を指す。bunchは「房」という意味。

220
butter
/ bʌ́tər /

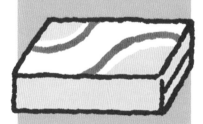

名 バター

Butter is a solid yellow food made from cream. You spread it on bread or use it in cooking.

バターは、クリームから作られる黄色の固形食品です。パンに塗ったり、料理に使ったりします。

□□□ **221**

jam

/ ʤǽm /

名 ジャム

Jam is a thick sweet food made by boiling fruit and sugar. It is usually spread on bread.

ジャムは、果物と砂糖を煮て作る濃厚な甘い食べ物です。ふつうパンに塗ります。

□□□ **222**

bread

/ bréd /

名 パン

Bread is a very common food made by mixing flour, water, and usually yeast and baked in an oven.

パンは、小麦粉、水と、ふつうは酵母を混ぜてオーブンで焼いた、とても日常的な食べ物です。

223

meat

/ míːt /

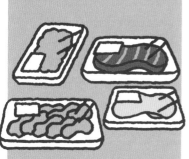

名 肉

Meat is the soft parts of an animal or bird eaten as food.

肉は、食品として食べられる動物や鳥の柔らかい部位です。

224

can

/ kǽn /

名 缶、缶詰

A **can** is a metal container which is usually used to preserve food or drinks.

缶は、ふつう食べ物や飲み物を保存するのに使う金属の容器です。

□□□ **225**

cash register

/ kǽʃ rèʤɪstər /

名 レジ

A **cash register** is a machine used in a shop, restaurant, etc. to keep money in and record what is sold.

レジは、お店やレストランなどでお金を保管し、売れたものを記録するのに使う機械です。

□□□ **226**

pay

/ péɪ /

動 ～を払う

When you **pay** an amount of money to someone, you give it to them for something you buy from them.

誰かにある額のお金を支払うとき、人はその人から買うものの代金として、その人にその金額を渡します。

✐ pay-paid-paid と活用する。

Scene

14

Restaurant

レストラン

server

menu

coffee

ice cream

tea

juice

cake

server

/ sə́ːrvər /

名 接客係

A **server** is a person who serves people food and drinks in a restaurant, café, etc.

接客係は、レストランやカフェなどで人々に食べ物や飲み物を給仕する人です。

customer

/ kʌ́stəmər /

名 客

A **customer** is someone who buys goods or services from a shop or business.

客は、お店や企業から商品やサービスを買う人です。

64

229

menu

/ ménjuː /

名 メニュー

A **menu** is a list of the food and drinks which are available at a restaurant, café, etc.

メニューは、レストランやカフェなどで手に入る食べ物と飲み物の一覧です。

230

curry

/ kə́ːri /

名 カレー

Curry is an Indian food of meat, vegetables, or fish which is seasoned with a mixture of spices. It is often served with rice.

カレーは、調合したスパイスで味つけした、肉、野菜あるいは魚を使ったインド料理です。多くの場合、ご飯とともに出されます。

📝 ここでのseasonは「〜に味つけをする」という意味。「カレーライス」はcurry and riceと言う。

□□□ **231**

pizza

/ píːtsə /

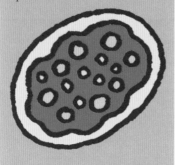

名 ピザ

Pizza is an Italian food made from flat, round bread. It is usually topped with tomato sauce, cheese, meat, vegetables, etc.

ピザは、平らで丸いパンから作られるイタリア料理です。ふつう上にトマトソース、チーズ、肉、野菜などがのっています。

✐ be topped with は「〜をのせる、トッピングする」という意味。

□□□ **232**

soup

/ súːp /

名 スープ

Soup is a liquid food made by cooking vegetables, meat, or fish in a large amount of water.

スープは、野菜や肉、魚をたっぷりのお湯で煮て作る流動食です。

65

233

salad

/ sǽləd /

名 サラダ

A **salad** is a mixture of raw vegetables, such as lettuce, cucumbers, and tomatoes.

サラダは、レタス、キュウリ、トマトなどの生野菜を混ぜ合わせたものです。

234

sandwich

/ sǽndwɪtʃ /

名 サンドイッチ

A **sandwich** is two slices of bread with layers of other food, such as meat, cheese, peanut butter, etc. between them.

サンドイッチは、2枚の薄切りパンの間に、肉、チーズ、ピーナッツバターなどほかの食品を層にしてはさんだものです。

□□□ **235**

ice cream

/ áɪs krìːm /

名 アイスクリーム

Ice cream is a frozen sweet food made from cream and sugar, often with fruit or chocolate added. It is often eaten as a dessert.

アイスクリームは、クリームと砂糖で作る冷凍の甘い食べ物で、しばしば果物やチョコレートが加えられています。よくデザートとして食べます。

□□□ **236**

cake

/ kéɪk /

名 ケーキ

A **cake** is a sweet food made from a mixture of flour, eggs, butter, and sugar, which is baked in an oven. Cakes are made in various shapes and sizes.

ケーキは、小麦粉、卵、バター、砂糖を混ぜ、オーブンで焼いて作る甘い食べ物です。ケーキはさまざまな形や大きさで作られます。

📝 可算名詞としては「切り分ける前のケーキ」を指す。イラストのようなケーキは some cake、a piece of cake などと言う。

66

237

coffee

/ kɔ́(:)fi /

名 コーヒー

Coffee is a bitter drink made from ground coffee beans and hot water. It is sometimes drunk with milk and/or sugar added.

コーヒーは、挽いたコーヒー豆とお湯で作る、苦い飲み物です。ミルクや砂糖を加えて飲むこともあります。

✐groundは「挽いた、すりつぶした」という意味。

238

tea

/ tíː /

名 紅茶

Tea is a drink made by adding boiled water onto the dried leaves of the tea plant. It is sometimes drunk with milk or lemon and/or sugar added.

紅茶は、お茶の木の乾燥した葉に沸騰したお湯を加えて作る飲み物です。ミルクやレモン、砂糖を加えて飲むこともあります。

□□□ **239**

juice
/ ʤúːs /

名 ジュース、果汁

Juice is the liquid which is squeezed out of fruits or vegetables and is often used as a drink.

ジュースは果物や野菜をしぼった液体で、よく飲み物にされます。

✐ squeeze は「〈果物など〉をしぼる」という意味。

□□□ **240**

wine
/ wáin /

名 ワイン

Wine is an alcoholic drink which is made from the juice of grapes.

ワインは、ブドウの果汁から作られるアルコール飲料です。

241

beer

/ bíər /

名 ビール

Beer is a bitter alcoholic drink made from malt and hops.

ビールは、麦芽とホップから作られる苦いアルコール飲料です。

242

serve

/ sə́:rv /

動 〈飲食物〉を出す

When you **serve** food or drinks, you give them to people in a restaurant, café, etc.

食べ物や飲み物を出すとき、人はレストランやカフェなどでそれらを人々に提供します。

243 □□□

eat
/ íːt /

動 〜を食べる

When you **eat** food, you put it into your mouth, chew it, and swallow it.

食べ物を食べるとき、人はそれを口に入れてかみ、そして飲み込みます。

✐ eat-ate-eaten と活用する。

244 □□□

drink
/ dríŋk /

動 〜を飲む

When you **drink** a liquid, you take it into your mouth and swallow it.

液体を飲むとき、人はそれを口に入れて飲み込みます。

✐ drink-drank-drunk と活用する。

ボキャブラリーチェック

本書で学んだ英単語を復習しましょう。
空所を埋めて、語義説明が表す英単語のつづりを完成させてください。
答えがわからない場合は、問題番号を参照し、
説明ページに戻っておさらいしましょう。

Savanna / Desert

サバンナ／砂漠

問題番号	語義

0 0 1　An e———————— is a very large animal with a long, flexible nose and two long tusks. E———————— live in Africa and Asia.

0 0 2　A z———— is an African animal which looks like a horse. Z————— have black and white stripes all over their bodies.

0 0 3　A l——— is a strong animal which looks like a large cat with golden brown fur. L———— live mainly in Africa.

0 0 4　A l—————— is a large golden brown cat with black spots. L———————— live in southern Asia and Africa.

0 0 5　A g———————— is a very tall animal with a very long neck and legs. G———————— live in Africa and eat leaves and buds on trees.

0 0 6　An o—————— is a very large African bird with a long neck and legs. O———————— run very fast but cannot fly.

0 0 7　G———— is a plant with thin green leaves. G———— covers the ground in fields and is often eaten by animals.

0 0 8　When you w————— someone or something, you look at them, usually for a period of time, paying attention to what is happening.

0 0 9　A c———— is a large animal with a long neck and one or two large lumps on its back. C————— carry people and goods in the desert.

0 1 0　A c————— is a plant which grows in the desert. C———— have a lot of sharp points instead of leaves.

0 1 1　An o———— is a small area in the desert where there is water and plants can grow.

0 1 2　S——— is very small, loose pieces of rock. S——— is found on beaches, in deserts, etc.

0 1 3   The s–– is the space over the Earth where you can see the sun, the moon, stars, and clouds.

0 1 4   When you r––– an animal, you sit on it and control its movements as it moves.

Jungle
ジャングル

0 1 5   A g–––––– is a very strong animal like a large monkey. G–––––––– live in African forests.

0 1 6   A m––––– is an animal which is like a person in shape. M–––––– have long tails and climb trees.

0 1 7   A s–––– is an animal which lives in trees and moves very slowly. S––––– live in the tropical rainforests.

0 1 8   A s–––– is a long, thin animal with no legs which slides along the ground. Some s––––– are poisonous.

0 1 9   A f––– is a small animal which lives both in water and on land. F–––– have long back legs for jumping.

0 2 0   A p––––– is a tropical bird with a curved beak and brightly-colored feathers. Some p––––––– can be taught to copy human speech.

0 2 1   The t–––– of a tree is the thick main stem from which the branches grow.

0 2 2   The b–––––––– of a tree are parts which grow out from the trunk and have leaves, flowers, fruit, or smaller branches growing on them.

0 2 3   A v––– is a plant which has very long stems. V–––– grow up and around something, such as a tree.

0 2 4   A c––––––––– is a large animal which has a long body, thick skin, and a long mouth with sharp teeth. C––––––––– live in rivers or lakes in warm climates.

0 2 5   A r———— is a large natural flow of water. R————— cross an area of land toward a lake, ocean, etc.

0 2 6   A b————— is a long curved tropical fruit with a thick peel which is yellow when it is ripe.

0 2 7   When something h———— in a high place, it is attached there so that it does not touch the ground.

0 2 8   When something such as a bird or insect f————, it moves through the air using wings.

Countryside / Farm
田舎／農場

問題番号   語義

0 2 9   A h———— is a large animal with long legs and hooves. H————— are used for riding and for carrying or pulling heavy things.

0 3 0   A c—— is a large female animal which is kept on farms for its milk or meat.

0 3 1   A s———— is an animal with long, curly hair. S———— are raised on farms for their wool or meat.

0 3 2   A p—— is a fat animal with a wide, flat nose and a short, curly tail. P——— are raised on farms for their meat.

0 3 3   A c——————— is a bird which is raised on farms for its eggs or meat.

0 3 4   A d——— is a common bird which lives on or near water. D———— have webbed feet for swimming and a flat beak.

0 3 5   M——— is the white liquid which comes from female animals, such as cows. It is used as a drink or in cooking.

0 3 6   An e—— is a hard-shelled oval thing from which a young bird is born. E——— are also eaten as food.

0 3 7   A m——— is a small animal with dark gray fur. M———— are almost blind and dig tunnels under the ground to live in.

0 3 8   A m———— is a small animal with a pointed nose and a long, thin tail. M——— live in houses or fields.

0 3 9   A f———— is an area of open land without trees or buildings. F————— are often used to grow crops or keep animals.

0 4 0   A p——— is an area of still, fresh water which is smaller than a lake. P———— can be either natural or artificial.

0 4 1   A f———— is a structure made of wood or metal supported by posts. F————— separate two areas of land.

0 4 2   When you p————— a wall or an object, you put paint on it to change its color.

Beach
浜辺

0 4 3   The s—— is the salt water which covers much of the Earth's surface.

0 4 4   A w——— is a line of raised water which moves across the surface of the sea.

0 4 5   An i————— is a piece of land which is completely surrounded by water.

0 4 6   An a———————— is a vehicle which flies through the air. A———————— have wings and one or more engines.

0 4 7   A c———— is a gray or white mass which floats in the sky. C————— are made of very small drops of water.

0 4 8   An o—————— is a sea animal which has a soft round body and eight long arms. O———————— are used for food.

0 4 9   A c——— is a sea animal which has a hard shell, eight legs, and two large claws. C———— usually walk sideways on land.

0 5 0   A t————— is an animal which has a hard shell covering its soft body and mainly lives in water.

0 5 1   A c––– is an animal with a soft body and a shell made of two parts which open and close. C–––– live underwater and can be eaten.

0 5 2   A d–––––– is a very intelligent sea animal. D–––––––– look like large fish but they breathe air. D–––––––– are often friendly toward humans.

0 5 3   A y–––– is a large boat with sails or a motor which is used for racing or pleasure.

0 5 4   When you s–––, you move through water moving your arms and legs without touching the bottom.

0 5 5   When you f–––, you try to catch fish with a fishing rod, nets, etc., either for food or as recreation.

0 5 6   When you s–––, you ride on waves in the ocean on a surfboard.

Camping
キャンプ

問題番号	語義

0 5 7   A m–––––––– is a very high hill, often with rocks near the top and steep sides.

0 5 8   A t––– is a portable shelter made of canvas, nylon, etc. which is supported by poles and ropes. T–––– are often used for camping.

0 5 9   F––– is the flames, heat, and light produced by burning.

0 6 0   When people c–––, they talk to each other in an informal and friendly way.

0 6 1   A l––– is a large area of water which is surrounded by land.

0 6 2   A b––– is a small vehicle for traveling on water. B–––– are usually smaller than ships and are moved by sails, oars, or motors.

0 6 3 A r————— is a small animal with long ears. R————— have long back legs for running and jumping. They live in holes under the ground.

0 6 4 An o—— is a bird which has large round eyes, a sharp beak, and strong, sharp claws. O——— usually hunt small animals at night.

0 6 5 A s————— is a small animal with eight legs. S—————— create webs to catch insects for food.

0 6 6 A c———— is a piece of furniture for one person to sit on. C————— have a back, four legs, and sometimes two arms.

0 6 7 A b——— is a vehicle with two wheels which you ride by pushing two pedals with your feet. B———— are steered with handlebars.

0 6 8 S———— are objects which you wear on your feet. They are often made of leather or canvas, and you wear them over socks.

0 6 9 A h—— is a piece of clothing which you wear on your head. H——— are worn for warmth, protection, or decoration.

0 7 0 A b———————— is a bag with two shoulder straps. B———————— are used for carrying things on your back, often while hiking or walking.

 Scene 6 Space
宇宙

問題番号　語義

0 7 1 The E———— is the planet on which we live. It is the third planet from the sun.

0 7 2 The s—— is the star which the Earth moves around and which gives us heat and light.

0 7 3 The m——— is the round object which moves around the Earth every 28 days and shines at night by reflecting light from the sun.

0 7 4   A s––– is a large ball of burning gas in space. S–––– can be seen as small points of light in the sky at night.

0 7 5   A c–––– is a bright object which moves around the sun. C––––– are made up of ice and dust and have a long tail.

0 7 6   A g––––– is an extremely large group of stars and planets held together by gravity.

0 7 7   A r–––––– is a spacecraft which is shaped like a long tube. R–––––– are driven by hot gases released from engines in their rear.

0 7 8   An a––––––––– is a person who travels into space and works in a spacecraft.

0 7 9   A s––––––––– is a machine sent into space which moves around the Earth or other planets, moons, etc.

0 8 0   The M–––– W–– is the pale band of starlight which can be seen across the night sky.

Scene 7 Body / Clothes
身体／衣服

問題番号   語義

0 8 1   Your h––– is the top part of your body, which has your brain, eyes, ears, nose, mouth, etc.

0 8 2   Your h––– is the mass of thin threads which grow on your head and body.

0 8 3   Your f––– is the front part of your head which has your eyes, nose, mouth, etc.

0 8 4   Your e––– are the two parts of your face with which you see.

0 8 5   Your e––– are the two parts of your body on either side of your head with which you hear.

0 8 6   Your n––– is the part of your face which sticks out above your mouth. You use it to smell and breathe.

0 8 7   Your m———— is the part of your face below your nose. You use it to eat and speak.

0 8 8   Your n——— is the part of your body which connects your head to the rest of your body.

0 8 9   Your s———————— are the parts of your body between your neck and the top of your arms.

0 9 0   Your c———— is the front part of your body between your neck and your stomach.

0 9 1   Your a——— are the two long parts of your body which extend from your shoulders down to your hands.

0 9 2   Your h———— are the parts of your body at the end of your arms which include your fingers and thumbs.

0 9 3   Your f——————— are the four long thin parts at the end of each hand, not including your thumb.

0 9 4   Your s——————— is the front part of your body just below your chest.

0 9 5   Your b——— is the part of your body between your head and your legs which is on the opposite side of your chest.

0 9 6   Your l——— are the long parts of your body which connect your feet to the rest of your body and are used to stand or walk.

0 9 7   Your k——— is the joint which bends in the middle of your legs.

0 9 8   Your f——— are the parts of your body at the end of your legs, on which you stand.

0 9 9   U————————— is clothing which you wear next to your body under your other clothes.

1 0 0   A s———— is a piece of clothing which you wear on the upper part of your body. It is usually fastened at the front with buttons.

1 0 1   P———— are a piece of clothing which covers your lower body and is divided into two separate parts for each leg.

1 0 2   A s—————— is a warm knitted piece of clothing with long sleeves which you wear on the upper part of your body.

1 0 3   A j————— is a short coat with long sleeves.

1 0 4   S———— are soft pieces of clothing which cover your foot, and often your ankle and the lower part of your leg. They are worn inside shoes.

1 0 5   A t—— is a long narrow piece of cloth worn mostly by men. It is worn around the neck under a shirt collar and tied with a knot in front.

1 0 6   A b——— is a band of leather or cloth which you wear around your waist to hold up your clothes or for decoration.

1 0 7   A d———— is a piece of clothing for a woman or girl which covers the body and part of the legs.

1 0 8   A s———— is a piece of clothing for a woman or girl which hangs down from the waist.

1 0 9   A n———————— is a piece of jewelry consisting of a chain, string of beads, etc. which you wear around your neck.

1 1 0   G—————— are two lenses in a frame, which you wear in front of your eyes in order to see clearly.

Living room
居間

問題番号   語義

1 1 1   A s——— is a long and comfortable seat with a back and arms. It is wide enough for two or three people to sit on.

1 1 2   A T— is a piece of electrical equipment with a screen on the front, on which you can watch programs with moving pictures and sounds.

1 1 3　A c------ is a cloth bag filled with something soft which you put on a seat to make it more comfortable.

1 1 4　S----- are a set of steps which lead up and down to different levels, such as in a building.

1 1 5　A t---- is a piece of furniture with a flat top which you put things on, supported by one or more legs.

1 1 6　A d--- is a large flat piece of wood, glass, metal, etc. which you move when you go into or out of a building, room, vehicle, etc.

1 1 7　A r-- is a piece of thick material which covers part of a floor and is used for warmth or as a decoration.

1 1 8　A b------- is a piece of furniture with shelves for putting books on.

1 1 9　A f----l--- is a tall electric light which stands on the floor. It consists of a tall pole with a lampshade at the top.

1 2 0　A c---- is a device which tells you what time it is. C----- are often hung on walls or shown on digital screens.

1 2 1　A p------- is a picture which someone has painted. It is made by putting paint on a canvas, board, etc.

1 2 2　A c----- is a round stick of wax with a piece of string through the middle which you burn to make light.

1 2 3　A c-- is a small round container, often with a handle. It is used for drinking drinks, such as tea, coffee, etc.

1 2 4　When you r----, you rest and feel more calm and less worried or nervous.

Bedroom / Study
寝室／書斎

問題番号　語義

1 2 5　A w----- is an opening in a wall, door, etc. which allows light, air, etc. to pass through it. It usually has glass in it.

1 2 6   C———————— are large pieces of cloth which you hang to cover a window.

1 2 7   A b—— is a large, rectangular piece of furniture which you sleep on.

1 2 8   A b—————— is a large cover, often made of wool, which you use on a bed to keep you warm.

1 2 9   A p————— is a rectangular cloth bag filled with soft material which you rest your head on when you are in bed.

1 3 0   A m————— is a piece of special flat glass which reflects images so that you can see yourself or what is behind you when you look in it.

1 3 1   A p—————————— is a picture of something which you make by using a camera.

1 3 2   A v——— is a container which is used for holding cut flowers or as an ornament.

1 3 3   When you s————, you rest your mind and body by lying down with your eyes closed, usually at night.

1 3 4   A d——— is a piece of furniture like a table, often with drawers, where you sit to read, write, work, etc.

1 3 5   A p————— is an instrument used for writing and drawing. It is often wooden and has a black or colored part in the middle.

1 3 6   An e————— is a small piece of rubber or a similar substance, used for removing something you have written or drawn with a pencil.

1 3 7   A n———————— is a book of blank pages, usually with lines, which is used for writing notes.

1 3 8   A b——— is a set of printed pages which are held together in a cover so that you can read them.

1 3 9   A d———————— is a reference book which gives information about words and their meanings, uses, pronunciations, etc.

1 4 0   A c———————— is a printed table showing all the days, weeks, and months of a particular year, which you usually hang on a wall.

1 4 1   S———————— are a tool used for cutting things, such as paper, cloth, and hair. It has two sharp blades with handles, joined together in the middle.

1 4 2   When you r——— something such as a book, you look at the words which are written there and understand their meaning.

問題番号　語義

1 4 3   A s———————— is a deep, round metal pot with a lid and a long handle, which is used for cooking food over heat.

1 4 4   A f————— p—— is a shallow metal pot with a long handle, which is used for frying food.

1 4 5   A s———— is a piece of kitchen equipment on which you cook food in pots and pans.

1 4 6   An o——— is a large piece of kitchen equipment which is like a box with a door. You bake or roast food inside it.

1 4 7   A p———— is a flat and usually round dish which is used to put food on.

1 4 8   A f——— is a metal or plastic tool used for picking up and eating food. It has a handle and three or four sharp points.

1 4 9   A s———— is a metal or plastic tool used for mixing, serving, and eating food. It has a handle and a shallow bowl.

1 5 0   A k———— is a tool used for cutting food. It usually has a sharp metal blade and a handle.

1 5 1   An a———— is a piece of clothing which is worn over the front of the body over clothes to keep them from getting dirty.

1 5 2 A k————— is a container used for boiling and pouring water. It has a lid, a handle, and a spout.

1 5 3 A l———— is a large, round, deep spoon with a long handle, used for serving soup, stew, etc.

1 5 4 A b————— is a glass or plastic container for liquids. B—————— are usually round and have a narrow top.

1 5 5 A s——— is a large open container usually attached to a wall. It is connected to pipes which bring water and carry it away.

1 5 6 When you c—— something, you divide it into two or more pieces with a knife, scissors, etc.

1 5 7 S——— is a white substance which is added to food before or after cooking to make it taste better or to preserve it.

1 5 8 S———— is a sweet substance usually in the form of white or brown crystals or white powder, which is used to make food and drinks sweet.

1 5 9 P————— is a spice made from dried berries, which is used to give a hot flavor to food.

1 6 0 O—— is a smooth, thick liquid made from plants or animals, which is often used in cooking.

Scene
11 # Garden
庭

問題番号　語義

1 6 1 A f———————— is an area of ground in a garden or park where flowers are grown.

1 6 2 A b————— is an open container with a handle which is used to hold and carry things, especially liquids.

1 6 3 A f————— is the part of a plant from which the seed or fruit develops. F—————— are often brightly colored and have a pleasant smell.

1 6 4   A s——— is a small, hard object produced by a plant, from which a new plant of the same kind grows.

1 6 5   The l———— of a tree or plant are the flat, thin, and usually green parts which grow on a branch or stem.

1 6 6   The s——— of a plant is the long, thin, and upright part above the ground on which the flowers and leaves grow.

1 6 7   When you w———— plants, you pour water on them.

1 6 8   A b—— is a flying insect which has a black-and-yellow striped body. B——— can sting. They live in social groups and make honey.

1 6 9   A b———————— is a flying insect which has a thin body and brightly-colored wings. B—————————— are most active during the day.

1 7 0   G————— are pieces of clothing which you wear on your hands in order to protect them or keep them warm.

1 7 1   A s————— is a tool with a rounded blade and a long handle. S——————— are used for lifting and moving soil, snow, sand, etc.

1 7 2   A s———— is a small animal with a soft body and a spiral shell on its back. S————— move very slowly.

1 7 3   A t——— is a large tall plant which has a hard trunk, branches, and leaves. T———— live for a long time.

1 7 4   A l——— is an area of grass, especially around a house or in a garden or park, which is cut regularly to keep it short.

Scene 12 City

街

問題番号　　語義

1 7 5   A s————— is a public road in a city or town which has houses or other buildings on one or both sides.

1 7 6   An i––––––––––– is a place where two or more things, especially streets, meet or cross each other.

1 7 7   T–––––– l––––– are a set of red, green, and yellow lights to control traffic, usually at a point where two or more roads meet.

1 7 8   A s–––––––– is a path with a hard surface at the side of a street for people to walk on.

1 7 9   A c–––––––– is a marked place on a road where vehicles must stop to let people walk across.

1 8 0   A p––– is an open public area with grass and trees, usually in a town, where people can walk, relax, play, etc.

1 8 1   A s––––– is a place where children go to be educated.

1 8 2   A p––– o––––– is a place where you can buy stamps, send letters and parcels, etc.

1 8 3   A m––––– is a building where interesting and valuable things, such as works of art or historical items, are collected and displayed to the public.

1 8 4   An a–––––––– p––– is a large place with many special machines which you can ride on for entertainment, such as roller coasters and Ferris wheels.

1 8 5   A m–––– t–––––– is a building where you go to watch films for entertainment.

1 8 6   A c––––– is a building which Christians use for religious activities.

1 8 7   A h–––– is a building where you pay to stay, especially when you are traveling. H––––– often provide meals or other services for guests.

1 8 8   A h–––– is a building to live in. It is usually used by one family.

1 8 9   An a–––––––– b––––––– is a large building which has several apartments.

1 9 0   A h———————— is a large building where sick or injured people are given medical treatment and taken care of by doctors and nurses.

1 9 1   A b————— is a structure which is built over a river, road, etc. so that people or vehicles can cross from one side to the other.

1 9 2   A h————————— is a type of aircraft with large blades on top which turn around very fast. It can take off and land vertically and stay in one place in the air.

1 9 3   A t———— is a group of railroad cars connected to each other and usually to an engine. It takes people and goods from one place to another.

1 9 4   A s—————— is a building or place where trains stop so that people can get on and off.

1 9 5   A r———————— c———————— is a place where a road crosses a railroad track at the same level.

1 9 6   A c—— is a road vehicle with four wheels and an engine. It can carry a small number of people.

1 9 7   A b—— is a large road vehicle, especially one which you pay to travel on and which travels along a fixed route and stops regularly.

1 9 8   A b—— s——— is a place at the side of a road, marked with a sign, where buses stop so that people can get on and off.

1 9 9   A m————————— is a road vehicle with two wheels driven by an engine.

2 0 0   A t——— is a car with a driver who you pay to take you somewhere based on the distance traveled.

2 0 1   A s————— is an underground train system in a big city.

2 0 2   When you d————— a vehicle, you control it so that it moves somewhere.

2 0 3   When you w———, you move forward by putting one foot in front of the other in a regular way and at a speed slower than running.

2 0 4   When you r——, you move with your legs at a speed faster than walking.

 # Grocery store
スーパーマーケット

問題番号   語義

2 0 5   A c————— is a long pointed orange root of a plant. It is eaten as a vegetable.

2 0 6   A t————— is a red, round, juicy fruit. It is eaten raw or cooked as a vegetable. It is often used in salads, sauces, etc.

2 0 7   An o———— is a round bulb with many layers inside. It has a strong taste and smell and is used in cooking.

2 0 8   A c——————— is a long thin vegetable with dark green skin and light green flesh. It is often used for salads or to make pickles.

2 0 9   A p—————— is a large round vegetable with a thick orange skin and large seeds. It is used as food and sometimes as a decoration.

2 1 0   An e———————— is an egg-shaped vegetable with shiny dark purple skin. It is soft and white inside.

2 1 1   G————— is a vegetable like a small onion with a very strong taste and smell. It is used in cooking to add a pleasant flavor to food.

2 1 2   G————— is the root of a tropical plant with a very strong taste. It is used in cooking as a spice.

2 1 3   L—————— is a large round vegetable with thin green leaves which you eat raw, especially in salad.

2 1 4   A p————— is a round vegetable which grows underground. P———————— are white inside and brown or yellow outside.

2 1 5   M———————— are fungi with short stems and round tops. They look like umbrellas. Some of them can be eaten.

2 1 6   An a———— is a hard, round fruit with juicy white flesh and usually red or green skin.

2 1 7   A l———— is a small oval citrus fruit with hard yellow skin and a very sour taste.

2 1 8   A p————————— is a large tropical fruit with thick rough skin and stiff leaves on top. It has yellow, sweet, juicy flesh.

2 1 9   G————— are a small green or dark purple round fruit. They grow in bunches and can be eaten raw, used to make wine, or dried.

2 2 0   B————— is a solid yellow food made from cream. You spread it on bread or use it in cooking.

2 2 1   J——— is a thick sweet food made by boiling fruit and sugar. It is usually spread on bread.

2 2 2   B———— is a very common food made by mixing flour, water, and usually yeast and baked in an oven.

2 2 3   M——— is the soft parts of an animal or bird eaten as food.

2 2 4   A c—— is a metal container which is usually used to preserve food or drinks.

2 2 5   A c——— r———————— is a machine used in a shop, restaurant, etc. to keep money in and record what is sold.

2 2 6   When you p—— an amount of money to someone, you give it to them for something you buy from them.

Scene 14 Restaurant
レストラン

2 2 7   A s————— is a person who serves people food and drinks in a restaurant, café, etc.

2 2 8   A c------- is someone who buys goods or services from a shop or business.

2 2 9   A m--- is a list of the food and drinks which are available at a restaurant, café, etc.

2 3 0   C---- is an Indian food of meat, vegetables, or fish which is seasoned with a mixture of spices. It is often served with rice.

2 3 1   P---- is an Italian food made from flat, round bread. It is usually topped with tomato sauce, cheese, meat, vegetables, etc.

2 3 2   S--- is a liquid food made by cooking vegetables, meat, or fish in a large amount of water.

2 3 3   A s---- is a mixture of raw vegetables, such as lettuce, cucumbers, and tomatoes.

2 3 4   A s------- is two slices of bread with layers of other food, such as meat, cheese, peanut butter, etc. between them.

2 3 5   I-- c---- is a frozen sweet food made from cream and sugar, often with fruit or chocolate added. It is often eaten as a dessert.

2 3 6   A c--- is a sweet food made from a mixture of flour, eggs, butter, and sugar, which is baked in an oven. C---- are made in various shapes and sizes.

2 3 7   C----- is a bitter drink made from ground coffee beans and hot water. It is sometimes drunk with milk and/or sugar added.

2 3 8   T-- is a drink made by adding boiled water onto the dried leaves of the tea plant. It is sometimes drunk with milk or lemon and/or sugar added.

2 3 9   J---- is the liquid which is squeezed out of fruits or vegetables and is often used as a drink.

2 4 0   W--- is an alcoholic drink which is made from the juice of grapes.

2 4 1   B--- is a bitter alcoholic drink made from malt and hops.

2 4 2   When you s---- food or drinks, you give them to people in a restaurant, café, etc.

2 4 3   When you e-- food, you put it into your mouth, chew it, and swallow it.

2 4 4   When you d---- a liquid, you take it into your mouth and swallow it.

INDEX

この索引には本書で取り上げた244語句がアルファベット順に掲載されています。数字はページ番号を表しています。

197

199

203

[編者紹介]

ロゴポート

語学書を中心に企画・制作を行っている編集者ネットワーク。編集者、翻訳者、ネイティブスピーカーなどから成る。おもな編著に『英語を英語で理解する 英英英単語 初級編／中級編／上級編／超上級編』、『最短合格! 英検®1級／準1級 英作文問題完全制覇』、『最短合格! 英検®2級英作文&面接完全制覇』、『出る順で最短合格! 英検®1級／準1級 語彙問題完全制覇[改訂版]』、『出る順で最短合格! 英検®準1級～3級単熟語EX』(ジャパンタイムズ出版)、『TEAP単熟語Grip1500』(アスク出版)、『英検®準1級スーパーレベル問題集——本番がラクに解けるようになる』(テイエス企画)、『分野別IELTS英単語』(オープンゲート)などがある。

カバー・本文デザイン：竹内雄二
イラスト：いだりえ
DTP組版：清水裕久(Pesco Paint)
ナレーション：Josh Keller(米)／ Rachel Walzer(米)
録音・編集：ELEC録音スタジオ
音声収録時間：約48分

中学英語で読んでみる
イラスト英英英単語

2021年7月20日　初版発行

編　者　ジャパンタイムズ出版 英語出版編集部＆ロゴポート
　　　　©The Japan Times Publishing, Ltd. & Logoport, 2021

発行者　伊藤秀樹

発行所　**株式会社 ジャパンタイムズ出版**
　　　　〒102-0082 東京都千代田区一番町2-2
　　　　一番町第二TGビル 2F
　　　　電話　050-3646-9500 (出版営業部)
　　　　ウェブサイト　https://jtpublishing.co.jp/

印刷所　日経印刷株式会社

本書のご感想をお寄せください。
https://jtpublishing.co.jp/contact/comment/